Mary McLeod Bethune's Cold War, Integration-Era Commentary

# No Room for Despair
## How to HOPE in Troubled Times

Compiled and Edited with Commentary by
*Talking Back to Today's News* author

## Dr. Carolyn LaDelle Bennett

PublishAmerica
Baltimore

First printing

Mary McLeod Bethune Front Cover Photograph
Courtesy of the State Archives of Florida

ISBN: 1-4137-9912-4
PUBLISHED BY
PUBLISHAMERICA, LLLP.
www.publishamerica.com
Baltimore

Printed in the United States of America

# Other Writings by This Author

*An Annotated Bibliography of Mary McLeod Bethune's Chicago Defender Columns 1948-1955* (2002)

*Talking Back to Today's News: An Editorial Writer's Public Affairs Journal 1998-2003* (2003)

*America's Human Connection: Commentary on Us* (1994)

*America's Human Connection* (1992)

*You Can Struggle Without Hating, Fight Without Violence* (1990)

Papers and presentations:
Journalism history and issues
Mary McLeod Bethune's columns in the *Chicago Defender*
Black Women and Journalism
News, Feature, Editorial Articles published regularly in:
*AIM Quarterly* Magazine (Chicago), *About Time* Magazine (Rochester, New York) *Buffalo Criterion, New York Beacon, San Francisco Bay View, San Diego Voice* and *Viewpoint, Philadelphia New Observer.*

Carolyn Bennett is a public affairs columnist and independent writer, educator, activist living in Rochester, New York. She has held print journalism professorships at Howard University, the University of Maine (Orono), Rowan University and other universities. She holds graduate degrees in journalism and education from American University (Washington, D.C.) and Michigan State University (East Lansing). Further background on the Web:

http://journals.aol.com/cwriter85/TodaysMissingNews/
http://hometown.aol.com/cwriter85/index.html

*In memory of my mothers*

*Laura Lou Pickett Bennett, Carrie Lou Stewart Pickett,*
*Laura (Ira) Stewart*

# Credits and Acknowledgments

Permission to copy, reprint and publish excerpts from and full text of Mary McLeod Bethune's 1948-1955 *Chicago Defender* columns for purposes of study, research, commentary and analysis was granted October 21, 1983, by Mr. John H. Sengstacke (now deceased), Chairman and Editor of the *Chicago Daily Defender,* and later, 2000-2001, by *Chicago Defender* Managing Editor Col. Eugene Scott.

Any changes in the previously published text have been minor, and only for the purpose of conforming to limitations of this collection of Bethune's writings. In the body copy—except where history absolutely forbids it—the words Negro and Negroes have been bracketed with the words African American and African Americans so as not to offend readers who prefer the latter terms.

Each chapter leads with an italicized summary of Bethune's thought. Words italicized within her text were italicized in her original columns. Quotations marks in the preface attribute her text.

McLeod in Mary McLeod Bethune's name is pronounced as in Loud, Cloud, Proud.

*I have risen from the cotton fields of South Carolina to found a college, administer it during its years of growth, become a public servant to the government and country, and a leader of women.*

—Mary McLeod Bethune cadencing like Sojourner Truth—

# Contents

Chapter 1    Preface    17

Chapter 2    LOVE THE LAND    21

Demonstrate Democracy    23
Never Turn Back    24
Extend Unity    26
Reject Rejection, Courageously    28
Demonstrate Idealism, Respect All Nations    33
Grant Full Stature    36
Choose Leaders with Integrity    38
Act Without Waiting for "Incidents"    40
Continue Under Flag, Constitution    43

Chapter 3    LOVE FREEDOM    45

Deem No Discrimination "Necessary"
Discrimination    47
See Human Not Race    49
Never Rest at the Oars    51
Do Right    55
Be Ready, Prepare to Excel    56
Shake off Race-based Vested Interests    58
Crusade for Integration    61
Burn Our Barriers    63
Work at Work Worth Working    65

Chapter 4      WORK FOR FREEDOM      69

Educate Hand, Head, Heart      71
Learn Character Crucial for World Service      75
Exert Single-Minded Effort      79
Demand the Best Not Segregated Education      83
Prepare, Break Through Fear      86
Jump in and Do: Hammer out a Silver Lining      88
Be Responsible for Self      93

Chapter 5      ENGAGE THE STRUGGLE      97

Stop Doubting Yourselves: Serve, Believe
You Deserve      99
Women, Unite for Peace      104
Women, Power Your Power      105
Women, Engage the Struggle      107

Chapter 6      MEASURE PROGRESS BY HUMAN,
                 SPIRITUAL PRINCIPLES      115

Choose Brotherhood over Paternalism,
Develop Common Cause      117
Reconcile      121
Revive Humanism, Know and Respect All
Nations      122
Know Right from Wrong      124
Choose Knowledge over Ignorance      126
Choose Better over Worse      128
Rise Beyond Race      130
Hunger for Spiritual Growth      131
Be Morally Mature, Don't Hate      133
Defeat Force Without Force      136
Don't Just "Stand For," Do      139

Chapter 7      POWER FAITH WITH ACTIVISM, HOPE          143

          Meet Challenges                                    145
          Fight Americans' Injustice with America's
          Justice                                            146
          Stop War                                           147
          Take Advice of Good Ancestors                      149
          Call on Divine Help                                151
          Break the Chains                                   153
          Give No Quarter                                    155
          Take Stock, Keep the Faith                         156

Selected Chronology
Mary McLeod Bethune 1875-1955 American Builder of
Institutions: Educator, Advocate, Activist                  159

# Preface

WE LIVE IN TROUBLED TIMES. Having squandered the post-Cold War era where peace was possible, we leaped from Communist scares to "terrorist" scares. Quite naturally we are afraid. An era that should have been one of prosperity—peace and progress, cooperation and understanding, reconciliation and reconstruction—sees us mired in terminal war. Instead of an era of equal educational and economic opportunity, we find ourselves mired in greed and separatism, retribution and malevolence, an era when cultural, religious, ideological, international, civil warriors and terrorist hunters tussle over power, leaving the rest of us hungering for true justice and freedom.

*No Room for Despair: How to HOPE in Troubled Times* advises humanistic, spiritual thought and activism. Faith with work. It excerpts from the thoughts of a woman who saw times like these, yet rougher than these times. What is compelling about her voice is that it is a wise and learned voice that general audience adult readers in America have never heard. Most people never heard of the name Mary McLeod Bethune, correctly articulated in three parts as one: "Mary McLeod Bethune," not Mary or McLeod, or Mary Bethune. Her voice is an old yet new voice.

The chronology at the end of this book gives a skeletal view of her life and contribution to America. The current book deals only with her thought—some of her thoughts—in troubled times. She was an American educator, activist, advocate and builder of institutions who was born in Reconstruction and wrote a newspaper column for the *Chicago Defender* during the period of the Red Scare, witch hunts, McCarthyism, U.S. House Un-American Activities Committee investigations, the Korean Conflict, the start of the Cold War, and Civil Rights fights for equal access and equal educational opportunities.

In a sense Mary McLeod Bethune educated those freed by Harriet Tubman. She saw the Klan close up in her day when people tried to register and vote. A hundred years ago she established the college known as Bethune-Cookman College in Daytona Beach, Florida. She was friends with Eleanor Roosevelt, and the only woman member of President Franklin D. Roosevelt's Kitchen Cabinet. She represented black women in work and pushed for integration in the U.S. Military. In the McCarthy era Communists hunters and scared "patriots" tried to smear her and hamper her work.

Mary McLeod Bethune stayed the course. In addition to schools and healthcare centers, she established and led women's organizations. A leading women's organization was the National Council of Negro Women. She traveled the country, as had women rights leaders before her and during her time, leaders such as Sojourner Truth, Ida B. Wells, Eleanor Roosevelt, and in the post World War II period, 1947-1955, Mary McLeod Bethune wrote a weekly column, as ER wrote her "My Day" columns, telling the story and advising people how to act and hope in troubled times.

The book title, *No Room for Despair*, comes from one of Mary McLeod Bethune's columns:

*Cease thinking of receiving and turn thoughts*
*toward accepting the wider responsibilities of life....*
*Don't quit or run away.*
*There should be no misgivings or lack of hope;*
*We need not doubt the intrinsic nobility*
*of the human spirit....*
*There is no reason to let up*
*No excuse for complacency*
*No room for despair.*

# Love the Land

*Mary McLeod Bethune's words were prophetic counsel when she spoke of America's relations with the world beyond U.S. borders, when she spoke of social injustice within the borders, and when she spoke of conflicts of conscience between citizens and their leaders.*

*The Cold War, military conflicts and the prospect of a third major military conflict she saw as part of a tapestry, a tightly woven web whose core was social injustice and disrespect for difference and human dignity at home and abroad. She saw social injustice and disrespect for other nations, peoples and different races as variables obstructing peace and disturbing the soil in which peace may be born and nurtured.*

*She believed peace was more than absence of physical warfare. She believed peace would be achieved when America resolved its conflicts with conscience: when America did what it professed, when it practiced its preachings, when it acted on what it stood for.*

*Mary McLeod Bethune called America to look clearly and honestly at itself, to recall its founding principles, and to demonstrate its innate courage by reconciling conflicts with conscience and laying fertile soil for peace with self, with all of its people, and with all nations of the world, without regard for differences in economic or social status, race or color, creed, ideology or religion.*

# Demonstrate Democracy

AMERICA NEEDS THE STIFFENED MORALE OF a people convinced that in war or in peace, all will share equally in the privileges of this democracy as well as in its responsibilities. The world, looking to America for democratic leadership, will turn a deaf ear to her pleas for democratic practice abroad, unless these can be demonstrated more clearly at home. Minority groups themselves can do much in this matter, with the aid of others who realize the political implications of world magnitude and the considerations of justice which are involved.

## Never Turn Back

AMERICA HAS REACHED THE POINT OF no return, the point from which there can be no turning back, in the struggle for civil rights.

We have carried on step by step and put milepost after milepost behind us, as we have fought our way forward. We have not turned back, but there have been times when we have been turned back in the struggle by the delaying action of appeasers and fence straddlers and accommodationists North and South, black and white. This has happened because of the tendency of minorities to cling to traditional political groupings, so that it was not too difficult to predict the direction of these voting blocs. Such a situation was easily exploited by political parties.

What is happening in American politics today writes high on the wall for all to see, the indisputable fact that the point of no return has been reached on the issue of civil rights, not only by the minorities who have suffered from discrimination, but by the major political parties and their candidates. Techniques have changed. Slogans have changed. The new term to conjure with is "uncommitted"—and the strength of that term is power in the hands of groups of voters as well as power in the hands of candidates.

The wish to exercise the freedoms, the civil rights associated with the word *American*, has set fires to old mores around the world. And in spite of the "realists" who would explain away the need for practical democracy in situations where it may prove to be inconvenient, America must recognize that she has reached the point of no return in civil rights, both at home and abroad, if she is to retain the world leadership necessary for world peace.

# Extend Unity

THERE IS MORE TO CIVIL RIGHTS than the declaration of a law. Something must come from the inner person, from the standpoint of the principles of justice and right. There must be a building of unity, regardless of sex, race, creed or color.

We must reach upward to the place where we can live with ourselves: to the place where we can analyze our relationships with other people—with other citizens—and find them sound and decent and tolerant and understanding and unpatronizing. We must be able to extend the feeling of unity that binds our households to the neighbors in the next block; we must extend our understanding to our entire community; we must study and understand our greater communities as the boundaries stretch away before our awakening minds, until we know that we do not want for ourselves that which we cannot share with our neighbor.

We must keep at our task of self-education until we learn that we cannot argue with God's law, which we must accept if we are honestly concerned with making the brotherhood of man a precept to live by and not just a text to preach by. We must develop unity and understanding in our church relationships, in our job relationships, in molding the minds of those whose hands will soon be on the helm of our Ship of State, guiding it through the storms of world disorder.

We must put into that fabric sound preparation and high standards of living and of personal conduct that will undermine the walls of blind prejudice and permit our neighbors to see us, as I trust we may see them, with open minds that accept the new order and work to perfect it.

# Reject Rejection, Courageously

MANY GENERATIONS OF AMERICANS OF NEGRO descent have avoided the pilgrimage to Mt. Vernon [Northern Virginia home of George Washington including slave quarters on the Potomac River outside Washington, D.C.] seeing only irony in journeying to a shrine of Freedom, under the stigma of racial segregation.

We know well that some of the Founding Fathers, including Washington and Jefferson, were sometime slaveholders. We know also that in the end they found slavery personally untenable and politically undesirable. We all know now that the nation which they helped to form has suffered frustration in internal affairs and embarrassment in international relations from futile perpetuations of race differentials, particularly when these are flaunted in the faces of visitors from other nations, as in the Mt. Vernon pilgrimage.

We may hope, I trust, that freeing the path to the shrine of the First President of the Republic [ref. to ruling against segregation on the

28

Wilson Steamship Line connecting our National Capital at Washington with Mt. Vernon], reflects a firm determination on the part of those who hold policy-making powers, to strengthen our national prestige by practicing at home what we preach abroad.

No nation is strong enough to incur, without positive hurt, the displeasure of many nations. Resentments have strange ways of making themselves felt. Those who bow to what appears to be unjust but immediately inevitable will be quick to resist when opportunity presents itself. We need friendship, not acquiescence. But friendship is earned—not imposed. And one way to earn friendship is by demonstrating the sincerity of our affirmations about the equality of humankind and the worth of the individual.

Through many of the recent years of tension and open conflict, we have hopped, skipped and jumped our international visitors, as they have done us, through selected areas of our American community, hoping that by skipping over those areas which would likely raise difficult questions, and by keeping our guests focused on evidences of our great resources, we could somehow keep their minds off contradictions which invite criticisms and raise doubts.

We have not been successful because we have constantly underestimated powers of observation and prior information among highly literate visitors. We smugly assumed naiveté on the parts of peoples different from ourselves. Our conceit has cost us friends and lives and dollars. That cost will continue to rise until conceit is brought down by an awakening of democratic responsibility and decent humility in our thinking about others of different races and nations. As a nation we are in the unenviable position of needing to prove our own acceptance of the freedoms of the Founding Fathers. Cleaning up the mass of contradictions on our national doorstep will help.

Racial segregation and discrimination are continual sources of embarrassment to the well-thinking people of this country. But of all the better thinking Americans who are deeply concerned about our national shame, the [African American] part of that group is the most embarrassed. Our [African American] leaders are embarrassed not for themselves personally but for their country: They feel deep sorrow and compassion for their country which has allowed itself to be placed in a vulnerable position on a question of morality. This is a serious question and our country must rise to its solution with the same spirit and courage and sincere intensity that has characterized its struggle in times of national crisis. For we are in a crisis. Segregation and discrimination cannot wait—it [the issue] cannot be shelved, while we wage an all-out "Cold War."

Segregation and discrimination are a part of that war. Our enemies have made it a part of the struggle. Our friends unfortunately share much of our guilt. But of all the countries of the world, friends and foes alike, the United States is in a better position to clear up the age-old problem of social injustice. Our constitution and our religious heritage force us to take a stand. We must make up our minds to LIVE the morality of our constitution and our religion. As a nation we must have done with constitutional evasion and religious hypocrisy. We must remove the burden of guilt from our national conscience.

We must do this as a nation—as one nation indivisible. No segments of our national life can endure the blight of segregation or discrimination. If these things are wrong within the boundaries of any single state; if segregation is wrong in New York or Pennsylvania, it is just as wrong in any Southern state. Morality and justice in THIS country are national in their interpretation and in their practice. On these two aspects of our national philosophy of government we must stand as one people before the world.

To do this we must live as one people in our homeland. The world expects this, for this is what we have always told the world. To live as one people in practice is going to take great courage on the parts of many. To live as Christians under our constitution requires that many of our citizens change their minds about a number of concepts of right and wrong in social living. And it takes courage to change one's mind. But what other choice do we have as a nation? We are a world leader in the cause of social justice. Our position as leader and chief exponent of and for social justice is at stake. Nay, the very cause of social justice itself is at stake. We are truly in crisis. Courage can bring us out of this crisis. Courage is all it takes—typical American courage.

American courage is not rash or ill-considered action. It does not mean running in the face of all historical experience. It is courage which involves the wise use of experience together with inner resolve to put idealism into practice.

Our country has been strong in the past because of just such courage. As a nation we have had a wealth of experience in the use of great courage. We have changed the face of a continent and spread our influence throughout the world. We have fed and housed the tragedy-ridden peoples of the world. We have preached the great unifying and participatory aspects of democratic government. We have preached the moral nature of democracy. Now the world is looking our way with questioning glances and embarrassing comments. Why? Because they see that here in America we have insisted on distinctions of race—in our schools, in our hospitals, in all manner of public facilities. They see that we have practiced it and preached it in our churches. They have heard the lesson of separateness drummed into non-white ears. Other countries, older countries, have established the same patterns among the peoples of Asia and Africa.

But what seems so difficult for some to understand is that few non-white people have given more than token acceptance of these views, and in that acceptance there has always been the hidden cost of mounting resentments. The lesson of separateness and inequality produced conformists, not friends.

31

With great concern [an African American] educator told me recently about a deliberate and open rejection of white students by their fellow [African American] students. The latter were heard asking, "Why don't they go where they belong? They can go anywhere. This is all we have." They were only students in training. But I say to you that we cannot train the individual with reasoning powers intact to think within limits—assuming that in a democracy we would want such a thing. The mind of the trained individual knows no boundaries. The student-trainee will not be student for long.

Azikiwe of Africa, Nehru of India were students once. The great Gandhi was still a young man when he was pushed from the sidewalks of Capetown. One remembered this when worldwide tribute was paid not long ago to the former Prime Minister of South Africa, Jan Christiaan Smuts, a great general. But from non-whites came only stern rebuke which denied him the name of statesman. For his name to them stood as a symbol of contempt for all non-white peoples. It stood for their rejection as human beings with intellects and souls and the right to human dignity. Heedlessly, unwittingly this man, who could have been a great leader of all people, limited his leadership and his power for good and paid for his lack of comprehension with his own rejection, in a time of crisis, by the non-white millions of the world.

Today we seek unity. We seek solidarity among all free peoples. But the virus of rejection has taken. It has multiplied many times the difficulties of our task. Loss of our freedom is too high a price to pay for the exercise of hatred and condescension. Freedom will stay. It must stay and grow and uproot the rejections!

# Demonstrate Idealism, Respect All Nations

AS THE COURSE OF OUR LIVES draws more closely to the lives of people in other countries and especially to the lives of people in less-developed countries where opportunity has been so limited, we must begin to recognize human dignity among all peoples, without regard to power or race or nationality.

Mutual respect and understanding are the price of peace between neighbors and nations. The casualties have been mounting through the years. People once friendly, here and in the far places of the world, have become cynical and bitter, frustrated and distrustful toward Europeans and Americans. They accept material benefits knowing that Europe and America need their good will. But there is reservation in the acceptance, punctuated by a question mark in their minds. Diluted applications of the concept of Brotherhood to relieve troubles at home and abroad will not work. There are times when we Americans are so lacking in decent humility in thinking of others that we actually invite disaster.

We brush off as bluffs the open and sufficient warnings of jittery, distrustful nations—because we cannot really conceive of any minor or underdeveloped country standing up to us and intending to go through with it. We brush off the suggestion that people whom we deem culturally inferior may become scientifically superior.

Lack of the spiritual sufficiency to take our beliefs out into the street and the marketplace and give them substance—failure to comprehend the need for a living Brotherhood—is pushing us, along with other nations, into a third major conflict. We are stockpiling the materiel of war, because we have not learned to recognize the material of peace.

The world is tired of patronizing "sops." The peoples of the world are neither so gullible nor so ignorant as to be unable to recognize, understand and accept the truth. The battle we are waging against Communism [insert today's anti-ism] is much more serious than many of us realize. In recent times we have done many things as a nation which would indicate that we have lost sight of our place in a "new tomorrow."

It appears that we fail to realize that every action, every spoken word, every consummated deed at home—on our own soil and within the confines of our own nation—is felt, heard, and weighed in many lands abroad. And one of the most serious areas of our national life is connected with our attitudes and actions which affect minority groups.

To be sure it is quite possible that a member of a minority group may be much more conscious of the things which affect the welfare of that group than those who are not identified with that group. But a patriot who is at the same time a member of a minority group may be even more conscious of national policy and national practices which, even though they may be deemed in the national welfare by some, are recognized by that patriot as critical points in international influence [Bethune was a patriot, close to federal government, and a member of a minority group].

We must remember that this time in world history is a first. This is the first time in the history of the world that such an issue has become a complete and recognizable pivot. The balance can swing toward demonstrated idealism. This is the one saving factor in the whole situation as far as our country is concerned. It is also the one danger point as far as the future peace of our times is concerned. It is time that we look at ourselves and realize who we are who sit at conference tables and proclaim a Christian-democratic idealism which we would have the rest of the world accept and believe in.

As a nation we do believe in our constitution. As a nation we do try to carry out the idealism of that sacred document. As a nation we do subscribe to the fundamental precepts of the Christian religion. But... We still maintain the Lord's Day as the most segregated time of the week. Eleven o'clock Sunday mornings is the most segregated hour of the week. These things we must face up to—face up to in terms of their importance as far as our own national welfare is concerned, and face up to as far as our own philosophies of government are concerned.

The battle against Communism is much more serious than many of us realize. It is a battle in which every active citizen and every soldier is an active participant. It is a battle in which the civilian can defeat the sacrifice of the soldier. It is a battle in which the issue may not be settled by conflict or cannon, grenade or bomb. It is a battle of the idealism of the minorities which shall decide the welfare of both minority and majority.

# Grant Full Stature

WHAT IS THE [AFRICAN AMERICAN] ON the street really thinking? With what kind of choices is he faced? Can he choose democracy gladly—strong in the consciousness that he shares in it fully? Quick as he is to scent the bait that Communism puts out to feed his hunger for full stature as an American—how secure does he feel in the democracy he chooses? How secure can he feel? What is his partial security doing to him? America needs to be thinking, now, about these questions because these questions that face her at home are the same questions that face the democratic world in its relations with Asia. What assurance of unfrustrated manhood and womanhood are we who expound democracy offering to the world to whom communism beckons? How free are our own dark-skinned millions? What seeds of frustration remain in American life, weakening the strength we seek to build?

Our resistance to attempted leadership by those who have become

bewildered by the stress of pressure against their f
blind us to the reasons for their bewilderment. ]
righteously indignant when an American of Neg
under the strain and seeks solution, either in
conformity or the grasp of Communist "manh
confusing it, in is need, with the food of freedom.

We are making the error of seeking to establis
bogeyman to frighten the world into friendsl
friendships are made that way. We in this country
and make friends in the East when we can show
region that the thousands upon thousands of A
[African Americans] in this country actually mc
freely as any other citizen within its borders.

How far—and how fast—are we being integrat
scale, in the executive departments and agencie
numbers? Not in token jobs? How are we faring ir
labor and management? How are we faring in hou
answer these questions satisfactorily, we will hav
effective answer to Communist propaganda.

The morale of a people is its [a nation's] first-

"W
The
dem
worl
we h
whe
V
lead
Leac
char
quali
word
O
enou
who

## Choose Leaders with Integrity

ARE STILL IN THE MIDST of a 'Journey Through Chaos.'"*
saving grace of what happens in America is that under our
cracy the people themselves have the room and the power to
their way out of their problems. We need the room and I believe
ve the power. I hope we shall be wise enough to wield that power
it counts most.

e seem to have increased techniques but decreased real
rship. The greatest need of our time is courageous leadership.
rship with integrity. Which means leadership that is
cterized by truthfulness, honesty, and uprightness. We need that
y which makes a leader a person whom we can trust, one whose
is his bond.

viously leadership requires intelligence, but intelligence is not
h. Intelligence without honesty is very dangerous. Smart people
lo not mean to do the right thing can cause much harm to the

unsuspecting. Truth is not just intellectual accuracy; it is moral honesty. A leader cannot make too many mistakes, it is true, but if the leader's mistakes are honest and are honestly acknowledged, he will be strong in spite of them. All that can be asked of anyone is that he intend to do right. Our very democracy depends on our trust in each other and especially in those who stand in the forefront of social, religious, political and economic battles. Here we must be able to believe we have good men and women.

Integrity makes a leader fearless. What has one to fear who has done what in his heart and in the light of Christian conscience he believes is right and just and honorable? The courage of leadership is faith in the right.

I cannot overemphasize the importance of leadership. There is now opportunity for young men and women who can hear greatness call. We do need courageous leaders, but leaders who will think circumspectly before expressing themselves in words or in actions. Young people must read the lives of some of the wise men and women of the past. Read in their life stories how they took their steps firmly and surely. Young people must broaden themselves by sensing the largeness of their spirits, for this is not a time for flippant, uninformed or narrow-minded guidance. Today's leader must be a careful student of history and have his finger on the pulse of current world affairs. It is not enough that he appeal to one group, but with a wide cultural background he must speak to all humanity.

## Act Without Waiting for "Incidents"

IT IS NECESSARY FOR US TO rededicate ourselves to action for a free world through united service—to break free from old errors that block the path to more abundant life for all. All of us are passing through labor pains that will bring forth a true spirit of brotherhood and fellowship and justice. It is hard for some to give up old traditions and alignments, but it seems to me that the harsh realities of the present are bringing us closer every day to the heart of a great problem of world restlessness.

It seems to me that men and women are beginning to see their own weaknesses and to recognize wherein lies their strength to overcome them. We must reconcile that which is workable with that which is right and just. The more accurately and fully all the elements of the problem facing us are understood, the greater the probability that they will be dealt with intelligently and adequately. The roots of our problems, the problems of the world, reach down through the layers of political advantage and disadvantage, through national rivalries and religious antagonisms, to things as fundamental as bread, clothing, shelter, and respect for the individual. And the last is the greatest factor which is fundamental to peace.

For there can be no brotherhood when men and women are forced to forego self-respect in order to get bread. When brotherhood is destroyed, so is peace on all fronts—military, economic, racial, religious. What remains is continued restlessness and conflict.

We have choices: between compounding old errors or breaking free of them; underestimating the minds and hearts of our fellow men, resenting and resisting changes that disturb old patterns or accepting the fact that readjustment and reconsideration are constant needs. What was done yesterday must be done over again today, in a somewhat different way. Effort must be unceasing, for every advance upsets some custom and interferes with some interest. But love is higher than hate, courage greater than fear and despair. Positive action is needed to support forward trends of thinking on matters of race, education and religion.

We must plan constructive action without waiting for "incidents." When incidents do occur, we must make doubly sure that every undemocratic act is promptly repudiated and corrective measures are promptly initiated—not to assuage the feelings of individuals directly affected but to set our communities back on the path of unswerving practice of equality for all, an American standard freed from blemish in the eyes of the world.

We must never forget that the American standard is the hope of millions. Too often it has been a standard of precept. Now it must be a standard of example. There is no other way. The days of preaching are over. America, and every other great power, must deliver the goods, without hedging. We must deliver the goods whatever the inconvenience—whether or not we lose an election and regardless to

41

what it does to our dollar profits. If our self-respect and the friendship of the world is lost, there will be few places for our dollars to go!

America has grown marvelously in the understanding of the fundamental oneness of humankind and of the need for recognition of human dignity among all people, without regard to power or race or nationality. American democracy is learning that the only way to peace is by a diplomacy courageous enough to forsake arrogance for service, domination for cooperation and the development and strengthening of human respect for all people within its borders and among all peoples of the earth.

To achieve peace in a free world, we must share not only material and spiritual strength, but life itself. As we look over the world today and realize the distress that is so widespread for want of peace through fellowship and understanding and justice among people, there must arise in all our hearts a desire to share, whatever the contribution may be, in bringing about a just peace in a free world.

We are called upon to share our minds, to take the time to be alert and informed and watchful of trends. And as we share our thoughts, we must take care that we evaluate past action, not in the spirit of carping or detraction, nor even in the spirit of negative self-accusation, but positively and constructively as a guide to action in the situations which we face today. As we sit down to our tables in our homes in all parts of the land, we are conscious of the needs of others all over the world, for food and for shelter. We are called upon to share our material substance. That is as it should be. The well-being of all of us is bound up in the security of those in the hills and valleys below us. We should come to love the "One World" concept as we embrace the older concept of national unity. This is the ultimate requirement of all who wish deeply within themselves that they and their descendants may live in the assurance of lasting peace.

## Continue Under Flag, Constitution

IT IS ENJOINED UPON US ALL, however varied our political persuasions, to continue under the banner of our own flag and constitution, fighting with renewed effort for all the freedoms vouchsafed to the country's citizens: for justice, economic security and brotherhood of the spirit. Thus can we advance to a rightful place in the leadership of moral nations. Regardless of where we stand or have stood in party divisions of the land…we must secure the oars. We can practice fine citizenship under any circumstances. We must continue the journey—moving not too slowly but as rapidly as possible, reaffirming an unwavering faith that each tomorrow will bring us nearer the goals we seek.

## Chapter 3 NOTES:

*A reference to Agnes E. Meyer's book concerning social problems and conditions, African Americans and children in the World War II era: *Journey Through Chaos: America's Home Front* (New York: Harcourt, Brace and Co., 1944).

# Love Freedom

*MARY MCLEOD BETHUNE SAID FREEDOM IS the absence of separateness. Freedom is feeling at ease anywhere in America—in schools, in churches, in work places, in public places and facilities of all kinds. Freedom is integration—freedom of association—not for its own sake, not for the sake of being with or merging with others, but for the sake of equality of opportunity, recognition and acceptance as persons and for the sake of a stronger America born of the unity of its people and the full utilization of its human resources.*

*This freedom should be denied to no one. And no one should fail to embrace it.*

# Deem No Discrimination "Necessary" Discrimination

THE AMERICAN PEOPLE MUST BE CALLED to a sense of values. Proper treatment of one's fellowmen is a matter of worldwide importance. What we do toward some affects all. A few people say desegregation is a "Southern" problem. That is not the whole truth. Desegregation is a national problem. More than that: It is a human problem.

The problem of discrimination against and segregation of [African Americans] retards the progress of the race as well as the international peace of the world. In every field of living we must push down the barriers of quibbling and evasion and align ourselves solidly against the forces of segregation and separatism that divide and imperil our democratic way of life.

I have been wondering just what kind of discrimination is *unnecessary* discrimination. Where it is permitted, discrimination in race and other matters does vary in the extent to which it is recognized by law or by custom and in the extent to which it is effective in state, local or federally administered communities. It seems evident that if the concept of discrimination is accepted at all, as it is by those who uphold it—it must be regarded by them as *necessary*. Therefore, all discrimination, in whatever degree, is what the proponents of discrimination regard as *necessary discrimination*.

It is amazing what can happen to principle and logic under the pressure of squeezing one's convictions into the shape of political needs, and what strange bedfellows are tolerated to insure party victory. Clear thinking and clean-cut decisions are lost in the scuffle for position. So many values are compromised that one wonders where victory lies and what substance it contains. Whether it takes the form of subtle distinctions insidiously woven into cleverly written laws or unabashed insistence on segregation in the United States or apartheid in South Africa, discrimination is always justified in the minds of its authors—as "*necessary discrimination.*"

Those who promise that there shall be no "*unnecessary discrimination*" promise nothing. They leave their hands free—and our hands empty.

# See Human Not Race

WHILE WE APPRECIATE MOST OF THAT which has entered our intellectual experience, very often we do not like that which we do not understand. One of the greatest foes of democratic living is prejudice, and the root of prejudice is ignorance.

We appreciate those whom we know best. But sometimes, while working in school, church or community groups, we are thrown with *other* persons and suddenly we begin to like something about persons we never did like. It is true that there is something quite different and quite likable about every other individual. I am grateful that God did not make us all alike and that His world is more interesting because each one of us is unique. Each has different abilities, different talents; each has unique value in the sight of God and the world. When we come to see what is good in another person, something not quite as outstanding in ourselves, we can appreciate that individual *for what he is*. This is part of the answer to the *Race Problem*.

Many of us have heard that there are great *differences* between White and [Black] people. This is what we might call a half-truth. There are great differences among all people. But the differences which set us apart as different individuals are far more than skin color or other factors indicative of racial origin. The list of differences could be endless. But when I encounter people, I look to see the human being, not the color or racial identity. And I find that our appreciations, our aspirations, our hopes and beliefs about important things of life are all much the same. Regardless to characteristics of color, cultural background and personality, there are likenesses which make it possible to refer to all of us as *people*. As different as we are as individuals, we are so much alike that we can speak of *the human race* and include all people.

It is the emphasis on the differences, instead of an emphasis on all that we have and all that we are in common, which makes for tension. Emphasis on our similarities, on the ways in which we are alike, makes for understanding and hence appreciation of each other. We cannot develop a peaceful society nor preserve democratic governance if the differences between our citizens continue to be more important than the common life we all share together. Our world cannot survive divided, segmented, segregated. The little barriers of difference can no longer be made into great walls separating humanity.

# Never Rest at the Oars

IN MY JUDGMENT THIS DECISION* IS the greatest mandate handed down by the Supreme Court since the Emancipation Proclamation. The basis on which the Court made its declaration was a great principle which runs deep in the heart of democracy: Segregation is Not Democratic. When the Court said that separate schools are in principle unequal, they were not speaking merely of physical facilities. They were speaking of human principles.

In a democracy, all people have equal rights. At least that is the theory. All citizens pay taxes, all share in the national welfare. In practicing racial discrimination we are not being democratic. And we cannot exist half democratic. Integration of the races in public education is the only democratic way.

Enlightened Christian people who have a sense of human values, who believe in world brotherhood and who have heard the conscience of America speak through the Supreme Court decision will work with zeal for the full implementation of the Court's decision.

We have possessed our souls in patience until this hour and will continue to do so until all the implications of this decision are worked out. We will unite our minds and hearts to help work out integration as peacefully and as harmoniously as possible. Of course we do not favor delay or circumvention. The longer our individual states wait to face the meaning of this decision, the harder will be their adjustments to it. Everything necessary cannot be done in one stroke, but it must be done. With common sense and constancy it can and will be done at last.

It is not the desire of the [African American] to enter "white schools" for the purpose of association with white people—just because they are white. We have great dignity and pride in our origins and in our race. We have contributed to the building of America, and we have a continuing contribution to make to American culture. What we want for ourselves and for our posterity is the best sort of schools, the best possible opportunities for development into the best citizens we are capable of becoming. We want that for all children, for all citizens. Not just for [African American]. Not just for White. We want Freedom.

Legislation is necessary, but it is not enough. When people who have been separated sit down to talk about their common aims and problems, the differences which existed or were thought to exist disappear. When people come together to discuss, to reason and to plan, the process of integration begins.

In many parts of the country, the reaction to the decision [*Brown v. Board of Education*] borders on hysteria.

We are not changing our constitution; we are merely taking a step to live up to the letter and spirit of our constitution. Our country has been engaged in building a great and impressive materialistic civilization, but all history demonstrates that no nation can long endure when it builds on materialism at the cost of moral responsibility. The ideals of state must be reflected in the day-to-day living of all the people. If we strive for democracy in world affairs, we cannot betray democracy on our own soil. The whole question of communism versus democracy hinges on the practice of democracy. All people of vision and objective perspective know this. To abolish the national sin of segregation and discrimination is to more firmly establish democracy—to set it on the high hill of world opinion without shame or apology. This is what we have wanted to do ever since we set out to combat communism on a worldwide basis. From this point of view the Supreme Court decision is an important milestone in our national history. It is another firm stone in the foundation of our country.

But the end is not yet. The Court decision is not the automatic end of segregation. To strive for democracy is one thing, but we can become so slack as to betray it. Unfortunately we still have those whose conscience and intelligence are so slack that they would not hesitate to betray democracy. They are the ones who, during the many weeks and months—indeed years—ahead, will fill the air and the press with hysterical words and hate-filled threats. But their children will be different: they have escaped this cancerous bondage; their eyes have been opened to the true meaning of democracy and they have come to see their country in historic perspective. These *emancipated* children of our internal enemies will grow in quality and number, but it is also true that their elders will continue to follow the *slave doctrine* of man's blighted past.

We must expect that the enemies who dwell within will do all within their power to circumvent the Court decision. We must not expect that they will accept full citizenship for all the people—just as they have been unable to accept the complete social doctrine of the church. We must be ready to meet their clever devices—for they will have many. It would be a serious and calamitous mistake for any person to relax vigilance in our struggle to build a moral state. More court battles will have to be planned and fought and won. More and more money and talent will be required, as will be more and more devotion to the cause of human dignity and national decency.

Let there be no resting at the oars! Let there be no undue rejoicing—nor hysteria, nor hate, nor precipitant action. Let there be no false security.

The Court decision was the only thing that could have happened under the constitution of our country. It was right. It was just. We must now go about the business of implementing the decision. This must be done with common sense and Christian forbearance. But it must be done! Within this simple fact lies the long road ahead.

# Do Right

FOR A LONG TIME WE HAVE lived under the doctrine of *separate but equal*. And you know and I know that while facilities for the education of [African Americans] have been improved greatly in many states in recent years, for the most part our *separate but equal* schools have been more separate than equal.

In periods of great social change, such as the one in which we now find ourselves, there will naturally be some spots where shifts in public opinion will not smooth. But we must never forget that ultimately the American people want to be on the side of what is right. The nation will not follow the early reaction of Georgia or Mississippi or Louisiana. If it were to do so, it would turn its back on the possibilities of future world leadership. If it were to do so, it would be insisting on a division among its people, separating us to be conquered by others. No. The American people will do what is right, and thus will America survive.

## Be Ready, Prepare to Excel

A FEW SHREWD "LEADERS" ARE MAKING the most of all sorts of propaganda and are resorting to some organized and quite questionable methods of pressure. Some of these on both sides are making the most of an idea that some [African Americans] "do not want integration" or "are not ready for integration." A few are trying to intimidate the [African American].

Of course any informed person knows that there are some who fear integration. We have all heard it said that some may lose their jobs. The few who do not measure up may indeed suffer setbacks. But the larger economic advancement which lies ahead for all our people—as not only schools, but all ways of American life open to us equally and without discrimination—will far offset this one aspect of the picture.

Let us not allow anyone to tell us we are "not ready." We have a right to question the authority of anyone who feels he may decide the "readiness" of his fellow citizens. In a democracy all are ready for their rights before the law. Decisions as to the worth of individuals are not made by other individuals. Beware of "fear control." Let us be careful whom we allow to speak for us. We must listen to our best leaders, those with the greatest wisdom. Let no man, black or white, say for the rest of us, "we do not want to be full citizens." History still speaks. It speaks for the rights of all citizens. And it will not be silenced.

Be prepared to excel. New opportunities bring new challenges. We are not only ready; we are not only prepared; we will excel. Unafraid, we hold high the torch handed us that we may help enlighten the world.

Respect and understanding come from constructive mingling, from the measuring of intellect and the exchange of culture, from free competition in mercantile and industrial development and employment, and from united community leadership. The day for this freedom to come to pass is here! We can no longer *get by* with lip service to democratic principles. The era of separation is behind us.

It is freedom of association, not separate but equal, that builds a strong American democracy—a democracy strong enough to withstand the pressures and stresses of a world in which pushed-around non-white peoples, subjected to all kinds of humiliating racial distinctions, have understandably developed unhelpful dislikes. Freedom and equality gives one faith and enables one to rise above impoverished beginnings. That is the faith of the free which is our real America—which must abound for all Americans, regardless of race, and to which we can point with reassurance for those across the seas—those who may never knock at the gates of our ports of entry but who daily knock at the gates of our democratic principles.

## Shake off Race-based Vested Interests

WE NEED NOT BE AMAZED THAT the growing pains of democracy affect us all. Nor that the wild weeds of discrimination spread into our own field, such that we fail to comprehend all at once—that integration is a two-way street.

This is a lesson some of us learned generations back. A lesson others of us have yet to learn: that healthy, democratic growth, of which integration is so vital a part, will not come painlessly nor without sacrifice. [African Americans] who protest discrimination are sometimes as guilty of discrimination as their white neighbors. Some [African American] preachers have vested interests in segregated churches. Realtors, both white and [African American], make easy money out of ghetto housing. Some [African American] teachers see benefits to themselves in being secured in positions in segregated school systems. Let us shake off every taint of such vested interests. Even if it costs some [African Americans] their teaching posts, even if it temporarily crowds out some [African American] students—let us no longer connive in any racial bias, said Dr. Edwin Embree in 1948.

Our segregated schools will one day be open both ways to all. Will we want them back? Our segregated jobs will be gone. Will we want them back? We have established some interracial churches. Must their pastors be of one race only? We who have suffered most from racial bigotry must fight courageously against it, wherever it shows its head. There is no easy, painless way to a full and functioning democracy. Integration is a two-way street.

One of the saddest results of the segregation of the races is the economic exploitation it engenders and the unhealthy clannishness it fosters. Pride of origin is one thing. Unrealistic racial provincialism is quite another. In our attempts to adjust to conditions often hostile and seldom better than negative, we have tended toward such an *out*. For generations we as a group have been driven upon each other. In self-preservation we have formed a square which we maintain for mutual protection. But no one can advance far in a square. Many of our handicaps still remain. They are handicaps which make it necessary to build businesses around a pattern of segregation. This makes us actually lean on segregation. It gives us a feeling of having done something for ourselves. We have done much for ourselves and for others. But it is easy to lose perspective under such conditions, and only human to measure results in terms of the effort which produced the conditions.

This is not to suggest that individuals should not try for participation as owners, joint-owners, managers or employees in a variety of business enterprises. What I am saying is that we should keep our own efforts free from arbitrary race restrictions. Rather we should help erase the lines that have shut us out from experience, from capital resources and, therefore, from larger economic opportunity. The time has come when we must dare to break the defensive square and

59

fall into position to make real advancement. As we resent the "for Negroes" sign on public facilities, so we must remove the "for Negroes" signs from our business efforts and from the names of our organizations.

# Crusade for Integration

NO PROBLEM SET BEFORE AMERICAN LEGISLATURES more vitally affects the welfare of our nation than the grave and imperative need for integrating all people—whatever the race or creed—into all the privileges, opportunities, and duties of full citizenship.

The eyes of most of the world look out from dark-skinned faces. We desperately need their friendship in our struggle for survival as a free nation. We have the dual task now of convincing hundreds of thousands of still frightened and appalled people: first, that integration is here and we will live with it; and second, that we will prepare ourselves to measure up to its possibilities—whether we are white, or black, or any other color. It is our constitutional duty to enter the doors opened to us. The idea that *we must take our time* is a false idea. The time has now come.

While we need not fall into pitfalls of violence—as indeed we will not—neither must we bow to complacency. Our stand must be positive and it must be united. Embracing the right, without fear and intimidation, we cannot fail. I warn my own people against any latent reluctance which may exist in the minds of any. I want to be sure we give ourselves to the full possibilities of our enlarged democracy. We need not be ashamed of being [African Americans]. We are full citizens of the United States. We belong to the world. We are members of the human race. We too are children of God. Let us stand together proudly with the best of our leaders. We shall soon discover what strength we have in unity and how just our cause really is. This is the way it will be achieved. Seeking Divine Guidance we will live together as a human family in this land, and we will grow in the spirit of living and working with each other.

It is not enough to help the [African American]. It is not enough to provide for him. It is the responsibility of the American people to welcome him, to respect his dignity, to treat him as an equal. In every area of American life—in every institution and in every section of the country—the [African American] is entitled to all the rights, privileges and responsibilities of full citizenship. Into some activities and some areas we may not care to go, but no other citizen should have the right to tell us we cannot—just because we are [African Americans]. It is illegal and un-Christian to do so. This is the realization of the American conscience today.

To say that one is not for segregation, but is not going to be a crusader is to say that one is not for segregation, but will not work against it. That one is for democracy, but will not work for it. That kind of "leadership" is devoid of responsibility to the people. Until we Americans acquire the courage to crusade for the American principles we talk about, we will continue fighting wars and losing friends.

# Burn Our Barriers

THE LAST HALF OF THE TWENTIETH century will be distinctive for the far-reaching propensity of peoples of the world to contend for freedom. There is abundant evidence of the desire for freedom, so it is well that we define freedom in functional terms. To live where one is financially able, to go to school wherever facilities exist for educational purposes, to go where other individuals go without first finding the right door or the right section in which to sit—these are illustrative of functional freedom.

I once heard freedom defined in terms of being able to purchase and eat a hot dog whenever and wherever one desires. This may appear oversimplified, but to thousands of individuals who have the money to make such a purchase the possibilities for gratifying their desires and the pangs of hunger are denied.

There are values inherent in this type of freedom. One of the values is that individuals live rich and full lives when they are endowed with personal freedom. If this value is of worth to a portion of the population, its extension to the entire population is self-evident. We know that freedom adds immeasurably to the good life, because we have observed the zealousness with which those who have freedom guard and defend it.

Individually and collectively we must search for torches to burn our barriers which separate humanity. The vertical hierarchy of superiority versus inferiority must be leveled.

Labors for the cause over the past years have been necessary. [And] in my judgment one of our most fundamental and urgent needs is the realization that integration does not come free, any more than did release from physical bondage. Liberty costs! Somebody has already paid in blood, toil, tears and hard-earned dollars for whatever liberties we now enjoy. Somebody *will* pay—in more toil, tears, cash, inconvenience and, not infrequently, with violence directed against them—for every inch of progress toward full democracy. That which has transpired is basic to the principles upon which leaders of today go forth. Integration in the field of education will be a great factor in bringing into being the day of total freedom for all people. To be at ease as a man or woman anywhere in the United States is the cry of the human soul.

## Work at Work Worth Working

WE ARE BLESSED TO LIVE IN a land which continually charges the human spirit with high aspirations. The ideals expressed in our constitution keep the American spirit pointed toward noble living and unqualified social justice. This attempt to live up to our national ideals and put them to work in everyday living constitutes one of the greatest struggles any nation has ever undertaken. No military conflict can compare with the wars we wage with our own national conscience. Our country has experienced bitter days in the fight for its soul. The spirit we see growing today is the result of a long struggle. It has been growing for three hundred years. And strangely enough our first struggle with conscience involved religious bigotry—not racial fanaticism. We have forgotten the days of religious persecution and how bitter they were. But the spirit of America is sound, and in the long run that spirit will cover all the land. Religious intolerance has almost disappeared from our land. Racial discrimination and segregation will likewise disappear from the national scene.

America must determine to build a strong structure of democratic practice on her foundations of democratic principle. It will take many bricks of performance, laid straight and strong and true, to raise the level of our structure of practicing democracy where it can be seen plainly above the rubble of failure and hesitation and face-saving gestures that have sapped morale, wasted precious time, and produced an inflation of the American ego more damaging to our national well-being than the inflation of the American dollar.

In too many cases the letter of the law has been used to completely destroy the spirit of the law. We must go at this business of equality of opportunity not by foolishly denying that color exists, but by working that much harder to see that equal opportunity prevails—despite color differences. Results will not come if we refuse to assemble data on racial participation as a gauge to further effort. What we must refuse to do is misuse such data for discriminatory purposes.

We cannot achieve equality of opportunity by wishing for it, or by saying it is already here. We who are [African Americans] must be on the job, inside government, seeing that the base of government actually broadens under present legislation or under such new legislation as may be needed to give life to democratic working. More of us must be on the job, seeing that programs are so equitably administered that the American who is [an African American] can, without prejudice to his own well-being, spend less energy and time watching for differentials based on race and devote himself, without reservation, to the common problems of all Americans. Let us work and pray and fight to multiply many times. We must help build a democratic structure of real performance—not as "an answer to the Soviets," but as sign and seal of America's determination to fulfill her obligations to all her people. We cannot sit idly by and hope for some "Good Samaritan" to thrust freedom into our hands. Freedom is something that must be earned, must be fought for, must be won! There is never a time for the people to sit back with folded hands, rocking in complacence by the fireplace of self-satisfaction. Now is the time to be out on the battlefield of civil and human rights. A handful of people have led the skirmishes, won preliminary battles. The decisive struggle is now on, and it will take unity of purpose and united action to win. Let us appreciate the progress we have made, but count it not as a goal in itself.

---

Chapter 2 NOTES:

*Reference to the 1954 U.S. Supreme Court ruling in *Brown v. Board of Education of Topeka* that laws enforcing segregated schools were unconstitutional and that schools should be desegregated "with all deliberate speed."

# Work for Freedom

*MARY MCLEOD BETHUNE YEARNED FOR FREEDOM for all people, and she knew that America contained the fiber from which freedom is woven. She knew that achieving freedom was no easy task and that all people would be required to enter the struggle for freedom.*

*She counseled that the cost of freedom must be paid by majority and minorities alike. Freedom is not a gift to be given by some and taken by others, struggled for by some, and enjoyed by others. It is a victory to be won by unity, sustained effort, hard work on the part of every individual in the society.*

*Freedom costs, she said. In order to secure freedom one can neither sit wishing it into existence nor stand waiting to reap the benefits of others' contributions—with vigilance sustained, one must engage in the struggle.*

*Diligently preparing oneself, taking advantage of every opportunity, and embracing service to all humanity as motivation and goal—this must characterize one's attitude and approach.*

*Education and training, regardless to the area or amount, must be "functional" education: it must be internalized in a way in which it produces positive changes in one's life and focuses upon constructive service to family, community and nation. Regardless to the type or level of work, work must be honest and characterized by the best effort, commitment, dedication, exemplary behavior. The purpose of work must be service to humanity.*

*Mary McLeod Bethune counsels America's youth to prepare themselves well, prepare hand, head and heart, in the cause of freedom.*

*She counsels the educated to make their education matter to themselves, and beyond themselves to others, in the cause of freedom.*

# Educate Hand, Head, Heart

WHAT IS IT FOR: What difference does education make—for you, your family, and the community in which you live?

Are you easier to live with at home and at work? Are you a better son or daughter, brother or sister, husband or wife, are you a better friend because of your education? Are you honestly concerned about the critical problems which face our society in this important period of human history? Are people important to you? Can you look on the person as a person, as a creature of God—regardless to the person's color, creed, status or faults? Do you desire to help others and be of service? Or do you put the matter of personal gain first in your dealings with others? Has your education served to make you want to be a person of integrity?

The use to which we put our educational opportunities is the most important thing. The individual who receives education has the responsibility to use it to contribute to the welfare and progress of the world. Education is a tool, an instrument. It is not just something to have, like many of our possessions. It is something useful; it is meant to be of service. Education for well-rounded living is never "completed"; it goes on and on, attracting and spreading knowledge as it goes. It pushes away nothing as too humble to be explored, developed and passed on in service to humanity.

Benjamin Franklin had practically no formal education, but gigantic intellectual powers with roots that went deep into the needs of his time. He seemed always to have realized that education is a process which continues forever: "Trying the mortar's temper 'tween the chinks; watching the cobbler at his trade"; and "the man who slices lemon into drink"*—learning from the humblest, never one-sided, never pompous, and therefore truly great. A great lesson for Americans of all races and creeds. I hope all of us will be able to see the courses from which real wisdom comes and realize that training and preparation in specific areas of learning are means, not ends in themselves, to the greater end of well-rounded living.

The days when we could depend on native ability alone are gone. Today we must acquire the skills and knowledge required by new opportunities. Preparation of the whole person has long been my dream for our youth. Training of hand and head and heart has been the aim of my educational philosophy. Manual, mental and spiritual development are necessary for well-rounded education. We must never lose contact with the real world of everyday tasks, no matter how advanced may be our professional or technical training. We must never lose sight of spiritual values: Good, clean, hard work is uplifting; it is an honorable part of living. It has its own dignity, carries its own rewards of great satisfaction—even in the humblest of services. As we find our opportunities in professions, in politics, in world affairs, we must be ready, with the full knowledge that these areas demand more specialized preparation. Academic programs should be built on a solid basis of developing the whole person. The person called to world leadership will be a person of broad training. The individual with knowledge of and appreciation for other peoples and their languages, customs, history and aspirations is the individual whose influence will match the hour.

> "The heights by great men reached and kept were not attained by sudden flight, but they, while their companions slept, were toiling upward in the night."**

To earn and keep our rightful place, we must work hard. We must be prepared for opportunities as they come, or suffer great tragedy upon entering a day of new hope with our hands empty.

This is the time for us to contribute something enduring and to take our place in world progress. The peace of the world for which all people yearn in their hearts will not come as a result of armament treaties or political compromises; it will not come if we "just wait." World peace must be built. World peace will be built by those who have human understanding, sympathetic knowledge and good will toward others. It will be the result of the cooperative work of those who have learned to work and to think, those who know the problems and have a feeling for the realities of life, those who have their eyes on life's spiritual meanings.

Our heritage prepares us to make our own contribution to the structuring of a better world. Out of our suffering and our sacrifice we can rise to assist in the righting of other wrongs. Our heritage gives us the full flavor of the grapes of suffering; we can approach world problems with a depth of understanding.

With more than ordinary preparation, the people of our race must rise to the occasion of our new and more nearly equal opportunities.

We must excel. In a land in which the proportion of college graduates is constantly growing, we must have something special—something that others do not have. When everyone else wishes to get technical education and the arts are neglected, when the demand is great for wealth-producing training, perhaps it is time for us to rise with a vision of service in law, medicine, ministry, nursing and innumerable other fields. If our people would turn to these vocations with a view not merely to making money but as ways of being useful citizens, we could make America vital and strong. Knowing what it is to suffer, we are prepared to understand suffering. Knowing what it is to be underprivileged, we are prepared by history to redeem others from want.

# Learn Character Crucial for World Service

CHARACTER AND INTELLIGENCE ARE REQUIRED TO render service on a high plane of performance. For the [African American], a special kind of character, combined with superior ability, is required to attain top performance in international relations. Character is a peculiarly individual thing, the result of an individual's conscious effort to feel right with self and with God. A goal not easy of attainment. It is especially difficult for the [African American] who dedicates his talents to the service of his country. Segregated, insulted by word and deed, categorized by reason of race, it takes a special kind of *character* to preserve any purity of spirit, even once that purity is achieved. It is difficult to fight for denied constitutional guarantees, and avoid a feeling of rancor. It is difficult to forgive in the spirit of the Christ, and yet remain militant in the spirit of Christianity.

The most conspicuous example of this kind of unusual character [was] found in the life of Ralph Bunche.*** He [was] likewise a striking example of superior ability. There was no magic at work in the life of Ralph Bunche; he spent years in study. All who would excel must prepare as Bunche prepared for his great task. The young person who aspires to be another Dr. Bunche must also resolve to dedicate his youth to study and hard work.

The [African American] who receives proper training is uniquely suited to the field of bringing peace to our country and to the world, through the field of international relations. But along with thorough training, the [African American] must possess strong and unusual character. The responsibility of secondary schools and colleges is to guide young people not only into those avenues of life for which they are fitted, but also into those vocations and professions in which they are needed.**** There is a social aspect of education which is often overlooked. There is also a practical component which must be the real concern of all of us. The educated man or woman should mean something to society. Future security and happiness in a chosen field of work rests on one's being needed. And whatever use society makes of the individual is determined by social need. Therefore, the practical and social aspects of education are mutually inclusive. As far as the [African American] race is concerned this mutual relation is indeed vital.

Education has become big business in America. We pride ourselves on our high educational opportunities and point to the public school as *democracy in action*. But in this bigness of educational enterprise, we must not forget the primary purpose of education: to make citizens who are not ignorant, who are useful and who have good character. An enlightened, law-abiding, moral, useful citizenry is the objective of education. It is therefore essential that democracy be practiced in the public schools. Here the child must see and experience equality of opportunity and find peaceful ways of living with other children. In this environment the child learns to live by living. Teachers should enter the school year prayerfully, with the attitude that this is a new opportunity to teach and act and live in a broadened democracy. And with full understanding that their challenge is to equip children to become citizens of the world. What a great privilege and what a grave responsibility is the teacher's task today! To have the reins of the future in one's hands is a grave responsibility indeed.

We educators and parents need to think more about *calling*. We need to be certain that we are guiding our youth in the direction of a real voice, not in the direction of echoes of superficial ambitions. Let us put everything we have behind a boy or girl who really wants to be a doctor, a lawyer, a teacher, an industrial chemist, a social worker or a banker and who has special aptitude for the calling. Let us also put everything we have and muster all the training and guidance necessary for a boy or girl who wants to be a cabinetmaker, modiste,***** bricklayer, building contractor, custom tailor, electrical engineer, road builder, radio technician, florist, or a farmer.

The curriculum builders in our schools and school systems, colleges and universities must look closely into the needs of growing industries. Curricula must be built with broad vision. We must renounce the silly snobbery of differentiation between academic skill and industrial skill—knowing that all skill well-taught, well-learned and well-executed is an important part of individual development and community progress—knowing that all phases of education are complementary and never in conflict. We must dare to point the way to vocational choice by aptitude. And through cooperation with labor and management we must relate instruction to actual working conditions in the field. And work to improve human relations so that young newcomers to the national labor force may be able to work side by side in shops, laboratories and on scaffolds in peace and understanding. We must have keener vision and the common sense and strength of character to work persistently in combining education for living and education for making a living into one harmonious whole.

It is now generally recognized that our youth need specialized guidance all along the way from elementary and secondary school on into fields of technical and professional training. But we must be certain that those who guide have keen powers of observation, adaptability, and common sense in the use of techniques; keen interest in and sensitivity to community patterns; and enough healthy brashness to undertake changes in patterns which restrict growth and thwart ambition.

We need counselors bold enough to advise students forthrightly according to aptitudes found, rather than according to immediately foreseeable chances of employment in a given field or community. [African Americans] especially need to hew honestly and ruggedly to this line. Too long we have burdened ourselves with job selection determined neither by aptitude nor by service to society, but by the dictates of the "Joneses" on the one hand and racial defeatism on the other. We have sent fine mechanics to medical school and made undertakers out of journalists, teachers out of tradesmen and lawyers out of artists.

We need parents, counselors, teachers and administrators who are alive and alert to what is going on around them; who are smart enough to assemble their facts and put them on the table for community judgment; and who are courageous enough to move out front and help adapt educational programs to fit carefully studied aptitudes into community needs and national and world trends. We should avoid resorting to educational speedups to compensate for time lost through inadequate facilities and unrealistic programs. Neither should young people be forced or advised to enter vocations distasteful to them or for which they are ill-suited.

# Exert Single-Minded Effort

I FEAR SOMETIMES THAT WE ARE making marks and degrees the alpha and omega of educational pursuit, rather than proffering as motivation the love of learning for the power of reasoning it develops, for the beauties it unfolds, and for the services it engenders when intelligently used to meet the practical demands of these strenuous times.

Are professors really encouraging resourcefulness, building habits of thoroughness, stimulating thought? Are they putting emphasis where it belongs—on the solid, steady performance that produces men and women of real worth? That produces founders of orderly, cultured homes? Interested workers for the welfare of their communities? Able representatives of communities in public office? We speak very freely of shared activity in world affairs. Quite properly we seek such sharing. But are our schools turning out young people who are familiar with the functioning of government at its various levels of operation?

I wonder sometimes what happens to the keys to effective living—between the early days of personal guidance and the later days when objectives and values become obscured, confused or non-existent. When information rather than knowledge seems scattered, superficial and unrelated to the basic facts of family and community life. When youth want to "get somewhere"—anywhere—with no thought of "paying for the ride." We must teach youth who sit in our classrooms and around our hearthstones that the keys to the kingdom of satisfactory living cannot be picked up casually along the way. For each individual these keys must be forged from effort spent selecting a worthy objective, and from labor of mind and hand and spirit spent reaching it. Whether the product is of mind, hand or spirit, it is important to concentrate on a single objective in order to turn out a creditable product.

In these days of much-doing, I sense a need for this kind of single-mindedness. Sometimes I sense a lack of determination to apply oneself to the attainment of a given objective—to see a definite purpose through to a satisfactory conclusion or to the point of a satisfactory continuing operation. A great many people of many races and many lands, from around the corner to across the seas, seem not to know what it is that they want to accomplish. Of the many who want *good jobs* in the field of education, most of them seem to be more concerned with acquiring an M.A. or Ph.D., in order to raise the figures on their paychecks, than to raise the quality of their service to a younger generation of students and to their contemporaries in community life. So many whose objective seemingly should be the preparation of youth for life make a display of their learning and the reason not for giving of themselves but for withholding themselves from youth who look to them for help and inspiration.

*I got mine, you get yours the best way you can!* Too often those hurting, arrogant words have been quoted to me by students who sought help in vain from a teacher who had failed to acquire human understanding along with book learning. One who sticks to the last, whether shoemaker or holder of public office and says, "This one thing I do" and does it—is going to be a success. In the midst of many interests one never loses sight of the goal—of the one thing, big or small, that one wants most to do and through which one makes a contribution to the times.

Mary McLeod Bethune in front of White Hall, Bethune-Cookman
College Photograph Courtesy of the State Archives of Florida

# Demand the Best Not Segregated Education

THE OCCUPATIONAL AREAS WHICH [AFRICAN AMERICAN] students enter after graduating from predominantly [African American] schools are governed largely by the courses which have been available to them as undergraduate students. Despite our best efforts, the limited curricula of *colleges for [African Americans]*—whether or not they bear that label—circumscribe occupational opportunity, even after the doors to employment are opened. This shrinkage of occupational choices is one of the most harmful results of segregated education, for it hems in our talents and makes good adjustment extremely difficult.

Under-equipped schools are forced to offer such courses as they have to many students whom they know to be unsuited for them. So we have students *dabbling* in areas for which the school can give no real preparation; we have graduates taking examinations only to find that their preparation is insufficient in spite of their degrees; and we have workers assuming tasks for which they are insufficiently equipped.

Counselors in such schools or systems are often faced with the unhappy choice of advising promising students, at the expense of interest and aptitude, to be *realistic* and select a course for which employment is reasonably assured; or suggesting courses in line with interests but inadequate in scope; or frankly advising students and prospective students to seek the desired training in institutions in which courses and facilities will provide full preparation for work in a chosen field. We are all painfully aware that this limited-choice situation begins its crippling action down at the youthful aspirations in the bud, insidiously molding youthful minds to conformist patterns in the determination and evaluation of their own futures. Much has already been lost to individual and society by the time the student reaches the level of higher education. Potential contributions to a revitalized society are so buried under the layers of accommodation to frustration that effective selection, even where available, has been sacrificed for *safe choices*.

We must move forward determinedly with closed ranks to open doors to full and fair preparation—for people of all races who are denied such opportunity. Without it, opportunity for employment can never be really fair. This problem of denial of adequate educational opportunities to [African American] youth in the southland is getting more and more attention today. And while I prefer that present schools for [African Americans] be made so efficient, adequate and unrestricted as to be attractive to any student—I would close the doors of these schools tomorrow, if that was the price that had to be paid in order to permit all aspiring, knowledge-thirsty youth their choice of attending any educational institution in America.

I am opposed to establishing any new segregated [African American] institutions designed to circumvent court decisions that are milestones of progress, but I am equally opposed to denying today's children the best available under the circumstances—while we who have passed school age continue fighting the Battle of Jim Crow. Theatres and other places of amusement can be boycotted, but we cannot conscientiously boycott education.

## Prepare, Break Through Fear

WHAT MADE GEORGE WASHINGTON CARVER *different*?****** He had a vision. He saw a *new horizon*! He worked hard to get the necessary training in his chosen field and then he went to work in his chosen field. He opened a door for his race. He pointed to a new day. That door today is swung wide. That new day is brilliant in the rich rays of opportunity and promise.

Julian******* and Hawkins******** excelled on the basis of their own contributions. They had the opportunity, they demonstrated their wares, and they have made it possible for any [African American] boy or girl to plan a career without fear.

To those who want to live dedicated lives, if a particular field holds your interest and you find and have demonstrated that your ability is superior, if this field of labor is your *tomorrow*—walk to it in courage, strength and faith. Expose yourself to the knowledge of your ability and choice. Excellence knows no barriers today. There are no denied tomorrows. Be calm and have a feeling that regardless to color, we are under a government which has declared that all men are equal and have a right to equal opportunities. We need only open all schools to [African Americans] and whites who desire to enter and have the ability to profit from the experience. Have no idea that integration will cause [African American] schools to close.

It is foolish to say that teachers won't find work if integration takes place. As long as there are children there will be a need for good teachers. If an individual is incompetent, he should not have a teaching position but should go into some other kind of work. We must not support the walls of segregation on the pretext of *job security*. To do this is to deny our children the highest form of education. There is but one real point in the struggle for civil rights for all Americans. That point is that full citizenship, the right of every American, is not something to be *granted* or *withheld*. It is not subject to qualification, nor can any citizen be legally set apart—by reason of race, creed or color—from the rights and privileges intended for all citizens by the constitution. There can no longer remain a question of *whether* any part of the nation will abide by our common constitution.

## Jump in and Do: Hammer out a Silver Lining

[WORK IS] THE DEMONSTRATION OF A spirit of duty measured not by minutes or hours, but by the responsibilities of the task that presents itself.

Some years ago I was talking to an older friend who was active in civic affairs and who had been conspicuously successful in the Midwest of the 1880s and 90s. I asked him how he got along so well in those days so much closer to the problems of Reconstruction.

"Well," he replied, "if we got along better—and I sometimes think we did—it was probably because we jumped in and did everything that others were doing for the general good, without waiting for *racial benefits*. There were many times when we made ourselves felt, simply as citizens, in matters in which race did not enter."

There must be *heart* in every effort. It takes organization and direction and enthusiasm to carry on—in sports, in politics, in education, in religion—in every phase of human effort. We will speed up achievement—when we make ourselves visible, vocal, parts of the activities which shape our destiny here in America.

I sometimes wonder if those who reap the benefits of solid, unselfish leadership realize the ceaseless effort that has paid for the privileges they enjoy. I wonder if they realize that there must be continuous, effective leadership backed by community organizations to keep the gains already made and to reach new goals. As [African Americans] and as proponents of good government we need to organize. We need to get back on the job. We need to reassert our power through improvement and civic associations—to command respect and use it as a bulwark between the economically weak and the economically and politically ruthless.

Competition is keen, but this should not deter us. The thing to do is to prepare, to qualify, and then dig in and work at any job available, until the opportunity for which we are ready knocks. If there ever was a time of emergency in this country, it is now. If there ever was a time for action by all Americans, it is now. If there ever was a time for [African Americans] to push aside weeping and wailing and defeatism, it is now.

This is the time to get things done! We shall find no silver lining to the clouds around us; that silver lining has to be hammered out, day by day, with persistence and know-how and eternal vigilance, on the anvil of our united efforts.

What we did years ago we can do today. For all the clouds of crisis we can go still farther, for we have the tremendous progress of those past years to stand on, as we move solidly together and reach ahead through coordinated thinking and prompt action.

From presidents and heads of executive departments out through the people and their organizations, we have the leadership. In the midst of national emergency we can achieve solid gains. But talk won't do it.

We must have higher caliber leadership in key positions of government to point the way, to help with planning, to help get things done. Otherwise what are we going to say to an employer of whom we demand full utilization of the nation's skills force, when we walk the corridors of government and find available skills of darker workers still underemployed and find others still waiting outside because suddenly budget appropriations have been exhausted, jobs have been filled, or programs aren't quite ready?

Preparation we must have. But there are thousands among us with all the necessary requirements, hundreds already available on registers—from stenographers and clerks to top-flight professionals, valuable professional and technical workers in their own right, regardless to their color or school affiliation. The few must be in there, working at the top level with all the other top-level officials. The many must be there in between, shoulder to shoulder with all other mid-level workers, helping to get things done, acquiring experience and status, seniority and security. Being Americans!

Hammering out a silver lining for the clouds around us is going to take all that. But it can be done. It has been done before. Progress for America in this time of stress is not going to come from the efforts of just some of the people. It is going to come from all of the people, working together. We have the challenge to wrest progress from crisis. We must have ACTION, now!

The time has come to cease thinking of receiving, and turn thoughts toward accepting the wider responsibilities of life. Facing squarely the problems which confront you is the first responsibility. Life is full of problems of various kinds and their solutions are necessary in order to achieve personal integration and improve community living. Don't quit, or run away from the struggle, or look to others to fight your battles. Summon from the recesses of your soul and from the heritage of the nation sufficient courage to stand and fight. One who is victorious must engage in the struggle.

Contributing to the growth and development of democratic government is another responsibility. Learn more about government. In order to play your rightful role as citizens in a great democracy, you must have a thorough understanding of the functioning of local, state and national government. Closely related to this: you must desire and be able to envision better government. Realizing the self is the greatest personal responsibility that an individual should accept. This can be accomplished by keeping one's mind on worthwhile things and on the pursuit of lofty ideals. Think, dwell upon constructive plans—plans for doing good, helping others, improving your community. Our nation needs more people who are thinkers and planners of the good life.

Engage yourselves fully in work. It matters little whether the job is one of high or low status. The dignity which you give to the labor and the honesty with which you discharge the duties are the issues of greater importance. While working give abundant evidence that you are dependable, courteous and efficient. Accept the demands of the situation, yet strive to improve the situation through orderly processes. Never stand afar and see the door merely open, enter and prepare the way for an abundant life of service to humanity.

Many factors enter into racial disparities in employment. In our attempts to make the best living possible, at one time or another, most of us have had to do battle with racial bias. What I want to point out is *how* we should do battle. Seek and create opportunities. Prepare for opportunities. Take full advantage of opportunities when they come.

Much rests with our community leaders, if we are going to make any appreciable progress. They should constantly recruit fresh energy and vision to leadership groups, find out the occupations of the people in their areas and to what extent [African Americans] are integrated into the general occupational pattern of the community. Unless a community is very unusual, race differentials will quite likely be found in both type and amount of employment. That is the first step. Finding

91

out what lies behind these differentials is the next step. It may be social resistance, so-called economic competition resistance, or it may prove to be lack of preparation due to one or both of these factors. The big job of communities is training and facilities: seeing that training and proper facilities are made available for all citizens and that those who can profit from them are taking full advantage of what is available.*********

The rest is up to the worker's initiative on the job. Often I am proud of initiative shown on the job. But often too I am discouraged by the *getting by*—the bare skimming of basic requirements instead of reaching up for a high degree of competency and achievement. Community leadership must knock loud and long to open the doors of employment to all. But it has the still tougher job of stimulating and alerting workers to take initiative themselves, increase their competence, and demonstrate their capacity for advancement in every field.

# Be Responsible for Self

WE WHO TRAVEL STILL UPON THE earth need to think of how the deeds we do and the services we render enrich the lives we have to take to the spiritual realm. We need to meditate upon the spiritual development and inner growth for which we are responsible here, so that our greater area of usefulness in that other realm may be multiplied.

The best that we have must be given in order that each one of us may know the joy of living, and bequeath it to our world. There is always danger in any thinking which removes or lessens in any degree the important sense of responsibility which every individual must assume. Only insofar as there is a change in human will, will circumstance alter its immutable pattern to fit the soul's dreams. Circumstance is the reflection of human will. Only when one wants something so earnestly that he bends every vestige of *his will* and every aspect of *his* ability—only then will one change wishing to realization. No new year can change the hard work that every man and woman must do on himself and on herself.

Of course I believe that there are great powers outside of and beyond mortal man. My whole life has been made up of a series of such discoveries and affirmations. I know there is a God and I know He answers prayer. Yes, there are powers beyond mortal man. But those powers may not be summoned with any success, until the person has used his abilities and directed his own spiritual energies to noble usefulness. When one year changes to another, we merely place an arbitrary point on the ceaseless flow of cause and effect. The placing of that point cannot change lives. Only a change in ourselves can change our lives. The whole grand mystery and magic of life is after all wrapped up in the individual life of each one of us. "As a man thinketh—so is he."**********

I fear that too many of us are looking to a date on a calendar, the day on which the Supreme Court hands down its decision, for example, as the day on which segregation will end. We must not delude ourselves. A victory at law is not a victory in fact. There is yet a great job to be done in this country. This major responsibility for the complete victory over segregation lies with the people themselves. That victory will not come as a result of magic—of time or circumstance. We must reawaken a deeper respect for ourselves as American citizens, practice good citizenship in all avenues of life, acquire the dignity that comes to a people whose objectives are high and whose conscience is clean.

Chapter 4 NOTES:

*Quote likely from a poem by English poet Robert Browning (1812-1889).

**From poet Henry Wadsworth Longfellow's "The Ladder of St. Augustine," 1858.

***Ralph Johnson Bunche, 1904-1971, born Detroit, Michigan, grandson of a slave, studied at Harvard, Capetown, the London School of Economics; became political science professor at Howard University, advised U.S. government on African strategic questions during World War II, won Nobel Peace Prize in 1950 for negotiating cease fire in 1948 Arab-Israeli war, went on to become U.N. undersecretary, then U.N. undersecretary general.

****If anyone one can be called an expert on education in general—and African American education in particular—it was Mary McLeod Bethune. From the time she started teaching in 1895 until her death in 1955, she had spent 60 years in hands-on education and advocacy. If you begin the count at 1904 when she established her primary school for girls, which she grew into Bethune-Cookman College, her years total fifty-one.

*****Modiste is a person who makes and sells fashionable dresses and hats for women.

******George Washington Carver, 1860-1943, born enslaved on a farm near Diamond Grove, Missouri, graduated with an M.A. in agriculture from Iowa State College in 1896, became director of agricultural research at Tuskegee Institute under Booker T. Washington in Alabama (1896-1943), produced hundreds of products (alternatives to the soil-depleting cotton) from the peanut, sweet potato and pecan, lectured widely on his work, was influential in the crop diversification that occurred in the South in the early 20th century. In 1953, the U.S. Congress declared Carver's birthplace a national monument. Ref: Schomburg and Chambers.

*******Percy Lavon Julian, 1899-1975, chemist, educated at DePauw and Harvard universities and the University of Vienna, Howard University professor, researcher with Glidden Company, 1936, founder of Julian Laboratories, 1953, adapted soybean products to commercial and medical uses, held more than 100 patents, developed synthetic cortisone used in treatment of glaucoma, elected in 1973 to National Academy of Sciences and American Academy of Arts and Sciences. Ref. Schomburg.

********Colman Hawkins, 1904-1969, musician, laid groundwork for modern tenor playing during the 1920s and 1930s, exploring chord changes more fully than any previous musician. Established himself as the most innovative jazz musician with the1939 recording of "Body and Soul." Ref. Schomburg.

95

*********Bethune had headed the Minority Affairs Division of the National Youth Administration in President Franklin Roosevelt's administration. She had established the National Council for Negro Women in Washington, D.C., in 1935 to help black women get good jobs in the government. She had worked with young people at her college, Bethune-Cookman. She had worked closely with white Americans of various professional and economic classes. She knew well the skills and attributes needed by workers in general, and African American workers and potential workers in particular. In her columns she spoke from a depth of knowledge and experience that is rare among columnists of any period.

***********"For as he thinketh in his heart, so *is* he" (Proverbs 23:7). *As a Man Thinketh*, a book by author James Allen (1864-1912).

# Engage the Struggle

*WOMEN AND PEOPLE OF COLOR CONSTITUTE over half the world's population, women alone over half America's population. Both groups are substantially relegated to lower strata of societies, and historically both have had to fight to obtain and maintain their freedom.*

*Both may be seen as representing the world's largest waste of human and national resources—because of underutilization of minds, talents, sensitivities and sensibilities; because of varying degrees of conditioning, internalized tradition and hesitancy, inertia, complacency, disunity, prejudice, and discrimination.*

*Each group says in one way or another we want freedom to be, freedom to participate in America's democracy, freedom to reap the benefits earned and paid for, to be accurately represented in media and in history books, to be recognized where and when recognition is due, to be respected as persons—as human beings, equal to any other human being, to have equal justice under law, to be at peace, and to enjoy their freedom to be.*

*All groups say they want freedom. But Mary McLeod Bethune posed the question repeatedly: Are women and people of color doing all they can to achieve the ends of freedom?*

*The ends of freedom, she said, won't come by wishing or by waiting.*

*People of color and women must, with unity and vigilance, enter the struggle and lead the way. Cease with petty strife and self-pity; clasp hands across lines of occupation, religion, sex, race, color, nationality, national origin—get into harness and pull.*

*Mary McLeod Bethune counsels those who have had least power to use the power they have, unite to secure their freedom.*

# Stop Doubting Yourselves: Serve, Believe You Deserve

THERE IS GREAT TURBULENCE IN THE world today. The war signals are out. The defense of democracy challenges all that is in us. Never was there a greater need for unity.

We have passed many milestones. We have made gains in integration—in education, in religion, in opening more areas of healthful living through the outlawing of restrictive residential covenants. [African Americans] have grown emotionally. We know what we want. We have learned how to *dig in* and direct our efforts single-mindedly toward our goals, without the aid of friends of questionable sincerity. We have acquired a tough independence of spirit that does us credit, and have learned to unhurriedly appraise professional sympathizers oversolicitous for our welfare. Recognition will come as we make ourselves felt fully, effectively, persistently. We have worked hard these years in the fight for democracy, because we need it so acutely. We have not received the recognition due. But we will not foreswear democracy, nor yield our loyalty to our country or our flag.

The struggle of the [African American] has one characteristic which I think needs pointing up. [African Americans] have always fought for *Principles*. Their fight in the past, as today, has been for the basic principles of the Constitution of the United States, the basic principles of Christianity, the basic principles of human decency and respect for human dignity.

The history of the American Negro has always shown a clear-cut tendency of the race to defend principle. If in the course of this defense we have been required to attack unjust social practices, it has been a secondary implement and a last resort in the defense of universal principles. For years we have defended the principles incorporated in the Constitution of the United States. We have been the *watchdog* of the American conscience—a task which seems to be our historic duty and which is still being carried forward with increasing effectiveness. For years we have defended and tried to implement the teachings of Christianity. We have tried to convince all people who subscribe to the teachings of Jesus that these teachings must be lived by all the people with all the people—that God is served only as man acts justly with his neighbor.

In the early days of the Christian church in this country we saw the basic principles of Christianity violated in a way which reflected on the fitness of the church to fulfill its mission. As a race we worshiped with our white brethren—but in segregated sections of the *hold* edifice. We knew this was in direct opposition to the teachings of the Christ. We saw the church as a hypocritical expression of Christian living, and withdrew from those churches which practiced segregation and set up our own places of worship. They were not buildings of grandeur or great beauty, but in them the spirit was free. They were not segregated churches simply because they were all [African American]. They came about as an act of defense—defense of a Christian principle.

Today the pendulum begins its swing back and we see signs, albeit far too faint, of the Christian church becoming the church of humankind, not the church of a race. We are beginning to get the idea that separate churches for separate races is wrong. One of the great hopes of my life has been to see salvation come to the church during my time. But as long as the Christian church maintains eleven o'clock each Sunday morning as *the most segregated hour* in the year, the Christian church will remain bound by a chain of hypocrisy that continues to choke off its spiritual vitality and social effectiveness.

In the field of education we have been waging a long and tireless battle of defense and at last we have forced basic principles out in the open. In a healthy society basic principles belong out in the open. We must continue to fight for principle because it is the only battle which is just and consistent with human decency and human dignity. It is the only king of battle that results in lasting peace.

In recent months one has heard conversations in which the question is raised: "What does the American Negro want?" And it seems strange to me that in this age there should be any question in the minds of civilized Americans regarding the Negro's desires for himself. As we look back through the years we see the strides that have been made. As our visions broadened the doors of opportunity widened for all Americans. The changes that have come about in the living and accomplishments of the [African American] tell their own story. There should be no inquiry as to what the [African American] wants.

Our movements and participations clearly demonstrate that the [African American] wants just what any American wants: *to be a part of his society.* The [African American] is a person—not a different or special or segregated person, just a person. The coloration of his skin does not make him any different, in essence. There are human

101

differences among all of us. But we do not segregate all the tall people, all the bald men, or everyone with blue eyes—so why make a special case of those who are darker (some not so much darker) than other citizens?

The American mind may need to undergo a little psychoanalysis at this point. We know enough about how the human mind works to realize that for too long the American people have been employing a *defense mechanism* concerning some of their number. There is no need now for white people to act toward the [African American] as though they were *compensating themselves* for the treatment given their black brethren during and in some way since slavery. In times of war [African Americans] serve their country, as do other citizens. In peace, they deserve the same privileges as other citizens. The [African American] gladly accepts the responsibilities of citizenship and wishes to enjoy its privileges too. The [African American] wants what all people desire: respect as a person, not humiliation. The [African American] wants *to belong*—not to a special group nor the classification as such. The [African American] wants to belong to the race of humanity. As indeed he does belong, but he wants the recognition in this country as belonging—as he is recognized in the rest of the world, a world in which he is not a minority, but the majority.

The idea of keeping the [African American] in restricted areas is unnatural and undemocratic. The [African American] wants to live free and unmolested in both private and public housing communities as do other Americans. The advantages of job equality, hospitalization, insurance and investment privileges should be the common property of the [African American] as well as of any other group in this great nation. The [African American] wants opportunity, not charity. He wants opportunity, not sympathy. The [African American] wants to be free to make his place in the sun.

The contributions which [African Americans] have made as they have found places in medicine, government, industry, education, music, art, science, sports, literature, diplomatic service and in the armed forces have been made with two strikes against them. Think of what our people could do if our society did not act as though the few who get through to the top—despite the structure's set against them— were *exceptions*. Our country will turn loose a whole new area of human resources when it fully frees the [African American]!

We look beyond the traditional line of segregation and discrimination to see a broad dissemination of green pastures opening where all who will may feed and grow and become—not [African American] citizens, but American citizens.

Stop doubting yourselves. Have the courage to make up your minds and hold to your decisions. Refuse to be bought—for a nickel, or for a million dollars, or for a job.

Don't be satisfied to ride behind the labors of others. We must work twice as hard as others do to find our places and to make a contribution to a new and better society. We must get into harness and pull together.

## Women, Unite for Peace

MARY CHURCH TERRELL, NANNIE H. BURROUGHS, Jane Hunter, Charlotte Hawkins Brown*—the leadership of great women, their untiring efforts, have made possible this day for the younger women who are finding their way to the front lines in all high endeavors of the world.

You must carry the torch higher so that the future may always improve on the heritage of the past. The cardinal principles for uniting women of all races, creeds and colors for better service to their day were established in the past. This is your inheritance. In this period of world tension and military threat to civilization, the womanhood of America is forging to the front. Women are giving their leadership and their full devotion in confronting the problems of injustice and inequality.

My mind goes to the opportunities that are opening up for [African American] women, and it leads me to call them with all my might to prepare themselves. Prepare for entrance into all fields and doors that are coming open and into whatever others may come open. Be ready!

# Women, Power Your Power

I KNOW OF BUT ONE FUNDAMENTAL way that we can be ready, and that way is through united effort. All women must pool their resources and abilities. Pull together. Unite for service and progress.

I have a positive attitude concerning what women can be, what they can do, and how wonderful our world would be if women would realize their potential powers. I am certain we can do greater things for our world when women call forth their powers from the mass heap of unorganized, ineffective activity and put their powers to work with victorious vitality. It would bring such joy and power to all of us!

We must unify our loves, our faiths, our energies and our powers around vital attitudes which yield cooperative action. Among us there are educators, psychologists, religious workers, scientists, health specialists and enough other specialists to help create the understanding necessary to make these vital attitudes the focal point for cooperative action. Women's organizations need to grow upon the *food* available in their ranks and expand those ranks to include the most humble women in the valleys and on the hillsides, by the highways and the byways.

I know the shuttles of the women will continue to ply back and forth, carrying the threads straight and true until the fabric is complete and women are solidly united in planning and carrying forward the work of the organizations—for unity, for strong democratic action, for peace and brotherhood the world over. The women know now that they cannot fail, there is too much at stake. The fabric they weave must prove strong enough to carry the weight of unforeseen burdens whose outlines and magnitude we now perceive but dimly. Women united will meet the test. They will get results. Women must move through their immediate problems into broader and more general problems, clasping each other's hands across the lines of occupation, race, color, nationality and national origin.**

Programs may differ, administrations will change, but the driving force of women united for service must remain the same and grow stronger as the years go by.

# Women, Engage the Struggle

IN MY JUDGMENT THE INFLUENCE OF women leaders in world thinking, together with the organizations they represent, can well be the turning point in the most decisive period of threatened war our world has ever experienced.

At the San Francisco (UN) Conference in 1945, I saw a great, common spiritual bond that could come as a dynamic force for good, if the great women leaders of the world would become more closely integrated in the policy-making bodies of the world and in the several national governments. When we think of the masses of our women who must be adapted to their places in the world and organized and united in their efforts, the challenge comes with great emphasis to every community, state and nation to call upon womanhood in whatever their surroundings to rise and become an active part of a great council of minds and souls. If women's groups could come together in a united effort, their combined intelligence and spirit and power would exert such an influence on international thinking that bombs and shells and all the devastating implements of war, together with the very spirit of war, would disappear from the face of the earth. A powerful spirit of peace and the nurture of peace would envelop our world.

I have always been a dreamer and I wonder as I write these lines if I am dreaming now. But these visions are so bright before my eyes that I cannot but speak them. Shall we not dream dreams? Shall we not have visions? And is a dream or vision of a way to peace impracticable? I think not.

All organizations which are founded upon and which foster humanitarian principles should dream of peace—especially those organizations made up of the women of the world. Their united thought and the power of their collective spirit can be a force for peace the likes of which the world has never seen or felt. I hope our organizations, in increasing measure, will begin drawing to them, women of all races, nationalities and religions—remembering that the place to begin is with the woman next door. Then we shall more fully prepare ourselves to work with the woman in the next state and the woman across the seas.

Women have had full suffrage for a full generation. President Woodrow Wilson issued the proclamation which became the Nineteenth Amendment to the Constitution, granting the right to vote to all citizens regardless to sex. It was part of a long, hard fight to bring full citizenship to all the people, for at the creation of the Republic women were among great numbers of Americans who were deemed unfit or unready for the franchise.*** Little by little these other groups acquired voting rights. Property qualifications disappeared—and this was the beginning of political power for the worker at the bench. Religious requirements were eliminated. Tax paying as a requirement for voting was wiped out in most states, although even today we see the remnants of die-hard thinking clinging to the poll tax.

By the beginning of the Civil War, most white men had the right to vote, and [African American] men were voting in some of the Northern states, mainly New England. Only women were still without this right of self-government, which they had been demanding since the 1820s and 30s of Andrew Jackson's administration. The women whose physical and moral strengths were helping to open new frontiers of thought, as well as new frontiers of territory, were asking for the right to cast their votes along with the men at whose side they had labored.

The tide began to turn in favor of the "Susan B. Anthony Amendment" which had been proposed in 1869 and which prohibited denial of the franchise on the basis of sex. Finally came victory.

Since then women have voted all over the country. Some of this vote has been thoughtful and informed. Some has not. Women of all races have helped to make a better America through what we now speak of as *political action*. In the years that have passed, [African American] women have joined with women of other races and of a great variety of national origins in building, through the ballot, an America capable of withstanding the terrific stresses of our times. As the women of America look back on the years of full status as voters, I hope they will think of the struggle and the heartaches that have put this power into their hands, and will use it, thankfully, to promote security at home and mutual respect and peace among the peoples of the world.

With whatever party they are registered and regardless to their choice of candidates, women of America must always lead November's marches to the polls! We must reinforce our efforts to unite for peace and prosperity, for brotherhood and freedom. Step to the forefront of this new campaign for political literacy and concerted action. Be very active teaching techniques of balloting and interpreting candidates and the measures they support. Women are people! Women are citizens. Gone are the days of walking behind brothers, husbands, fathers, employers or preachers. Women are at least as discerning as men. They are at least as thorough. They are at least as objective. In thought and action, they are competitive as people, *but as people who are also women.* In addition to the overall problems of local and national communities, there are specific areas of action which claim the particular interest of women.

We must key our minds to the problems of the day: analyze, select, discard, and act. Effort? Of course it takes effort! The pioneer women worked as hard as the men. They worked with the men. We must do likewise. Often we will have to take the initiative in exploring problems, suggesting action, checking records. Women must do the research: find out what candidates are saying and doing, what they have and have not done.\*\*\*\* Women must be informed voters and must help to inform others. They must find out how to vote—then vote. That is their function as citizens. If we are not too busy to live, then we cannot be too busy to understand and help direct the manner of our living.

[Helen Keller] is an inspiration to thousands because she was not content to sit back and pity herself. Robbed of sight, hearing and speech, she refused to allow these handicaps to keep her from making a contribution to humanity. Helen Keller did something about her handicaps.\*\*\*\*\* I can think of no greater challenge to the womanhood of our race. We too have handicaps. But are we doing everything we can to overcome them? Though we have the sight of two good eyes, are we blind to the opportunities for service incumbent in strong organization and zealous work? Though we have our hearing, are we deaf to the call of duty? It is our duty to light the way to love and understanding and neighborliness among people, communities and nations. Though we have our speech, are we mute when we should speak out? What are we doing to make Members of Congress and

Senators know how we want them to vote on housing legislation, federal aid to education, minimum wages, equitable labor legislation, national health bills and firm, peace-seeking foreign policy? What are we doing to make these same Members of Congress and Senators aware of our desires in the field of civil rights? Banded together our women could be such a superior force in the battle for world peace, democracy and civil rights that victory would be swift and sure.

Great areas of tension still exist in our world. But the powers of united women are coming courageously to the rescue. Women are entering fields of religion, education, business, government and carrying forward the great procession of life with patience and fortitude. The works of outstanding women, such as Eleanor Roosevelt****** and Madam Pandit,******* in building world understanding are signs of promise that God has regarded the lowly estate of women and has given them the spiritual understanding with which to bless the world.

No wise leader ignores the strength of women!

---

Chapter 5 NOTES:

*All Bethune contemporaries. Mary Eliza Church Terrell (1863-1954) was born in Memphis, Tennessee, as the Civil War was ending. She became a leading 20th century activist, championing equality for women and black Americans. In 1896, Terrell founded and led the National Association of Colored Women which established homes for girls, the aged and the sick. She wrote articles and short stories on lynching, chain gangs and disfranchisement of African Americans. In her final years she turned her militancy against segregation in eating places in Washington, D.C., and won the fight. Nannie Helen Burroughs (1879-1961) was born in Orange,

Virginia. She was a religious leader, educator, club woman, political organizer, and civil rights activist. Her crowning achievements were articulating the discontent of women to the Black Baptist church and leading the way toward formation of the largest Black women's organization in America—the Woman's Convention Auxiliary to the National Baptist Convention; and, in 1909, establishing the National Training School for Women and Girls in Washington. D.C. Jane Hunter (1882-1971) was born on the Woodburn Plantation near Pendleton, South Carolina, and started her career as a nurse. Later she established and was executive director of the Phillis Wheatley Association in Cleveland, Ohio, an independent association that, in 1913, opened its first home for Black women. It became the model for a network of clubs, residences, and employment services throughout the United States. Charlotte Hawkins Brown (1883-1961) was born in Henderson, North Carolina, and was a major force in the educational and club work of early 20th century African American women. She studied at normal schools and at Harvard in summers. Her crowning achievement was the establishment of the Palmer Memorial Institute, a finishing school with lessons in fighting civil rights and injustice, in Sedalia, North Carolina. She was also among the founding members of Bethune's National Council of Negro Women. Ref. *Black Women in America*, Hine, Brown and Terborg-Penn.

**Bethune worked with the women's club movement early in the 20th century and founded the National Council of Negro Women, a collection of African American women's groups, in Washington, D.C., in 1935. She was influential in and through the NCNW for the rest of her life. A full chronology follows the main body of text.

***The 1920 ratification of the Nineteenth Amendment to the U.S. Constitution gave women the right to vote, but in the early period of the suffrage Amendment, Bethune had to confront the Klan to register women to vote in Daytona Beach, Florida; and most African Americans were unable to vote in the U.S. until enactment of the Civil Rights Act of 1960 and the Voting Rights Act of 1965 followed by Federal courts' prohibition of the last poll tax in 1966.

****The League of Women Voters was founded the year the Woman Suffrage Amendment was ratified.

*****Helen Adams Keller (1880-1968) was born in Tuscumbia, Alabama, and lost her hearing and sight when she was 19 months old. She was unable to communicate through language until she was 7 years old. After being taught by Anne M. Sullivan, she learned to use sign language and to speak. In 1904, she graduated from Radcliffe College and subsequently became a famous lecturer and crusader for the handicapped. She published several books based on her experiences. Ref. Chambers.

******Anna Eleanor Roosevelt (1884-1962) was among Mary McLeod Bethune's

112

friends. They appeared often on the same stages championing the same causes. Eleanor Roosevelt was an American diplomat, humanitarian, and First Lady of the United States. She is best known for her work on behalf of women, children, the poor, and African Americans. After President Franklin Roosevelt's death she became American delegate to the United Nations (1946), then chairman of the UN Human Rights Commission (1947-1952) and was instrumental in creating the 1948 Universal Declaration of Human Rights. From the 1930s until her death, she wrote a newspaper column "My Day." She advised presidents and spoke widely on human rights and justice. Ref: *Who's Who of Women in the Twentieth Century.*

*******Vijaya Lakshmi Pandit (1900-1990) was Indian freedom fighter, politician and diplomat. She was the first woman president of the UN General Assembly (1953). She championed the cause of Indian independence and after its independence in 1947 she became ambassador to the USSR (1947-49), then the U.S. (1949-1951), then High Commissioner to Britain (1955-61). She was sister to India's first prime minister of independent India, Jawaharlal Nehru. Ref: *Who's Who of Women in the Twentieth Century.*

# Measure Progress by Human, Spiritual Principles

*WHILE MARY MCLEOD BETHUNE KNEW WELL and commented extensively on the problems in America—problems of segregation and discrimination, prejudice and bigotry, complacency and passive consent to social injustice on the parts of government, organizations, institutions, churches and individuals—she never failed to hope. She never failed to believe in herself, in the founding principles of America's democracy, and in the principles of brotherhood.*

*In her view, important principles to be used in measuring human progress were principles in the human-to-human relationship, "brotherhood," and in the religion she practiced, ethics imbedded in Christian texts. Hers were principles of humanism combined with humanitarianism, holding to fundamental concerns for the dignity of individuals and respect for persons as persons. Principles concerned with human welfare, society, social reform when reform becomes necessary to correct wrongs imposed by a society on the individual, or by individuals or institutions on some members of society. Principles of unity and inter-faith activism for the common good.*

*Mary McLeod Bethune knew that America was not devoid of principle. She believed that the problems of injustice in America were rooted in America's "conflicts with conscience." She believed America's acts were in violation of her principles. That there were conflicts between preachments and practices, between stands and doings, between founding principles "under God," espoused principles of freedom and democracy, and overt violations of human rights; failure to live principles of brotherhood, to respect persons, and to appreciate difference at home and abroad. America is "stockpiling the materiel of war," she said, "because she fails to recognize the material of peace."*

*Mary McLeod Bethune saw issues of segregation and discrimination, war and absence of peace as having the same root: "Conflict of Conscience." To her these were moral issues requiring moral solutions. "The whole story of segregation and discrimination is a recitation of inconsistency and compromise of conscience." The issues of segregation and discrimination (by virtue of the color of skin and a former cast condition of legalized slavery), are "basically moral issues...they involve the moral sense of our country."*

*Because they are moral issues, "America must mobilize spiritual resources" to confront them.*

# Choose Brotherhood over Paternalism,
## Develop Common Cause

OUR GREAT UNITED STATES IS FREE today because *We the People* subscribe ourselves to great revolutions of thought and progress. We examine the affairs of men and pledge ourselves year after year to some of the ideals to which we ascribe our efforts in order that they may become realities. We have spoken of enrichment and equal opportunity for all races, creeds, cultures, colors and nationalities. Finally, in this crucial era of our existence, we have come to the one word that embodies all our feelings. The word is *Brotherhood.*

Because we have solved so many of our problems of physical existence and, in a material sense, are weary with our overabundance, we have come to realize the loneliness of our hearts. We have discovered that in the final breaths of sons, sweethearts, husbands and fathers, a feeble hand stretches forth and the whisper is, "Brother." Brotherhood does not come through academic instruction or the writing of great speeches. It grows out of a spirit of love yielding justice, and equality, and fair play. It unfolds the best that inheres in man, woman or institution. The act of brotherhood begins with an open mind: an openness to appreciate all nations of the earth, their different ways of working and worshiping, governing and enjoying life.

As we talk much about democracy, equal opportunities, brotherhood, let us *do* brotherhood: begin to unite our minds and work at the ideal upon which our nation is founded. Let us do this before lesser ideologies rise up to put us to shame and drive us into chaos.

I have a deep and abiding belief in a religion that teaches brotherhood. I also know that the teaching is only meaningful as we breathe life into it; it is only meaningful as we apply it to every action of our days. I believe our lack of spiritual sufficiency to take our beliefs and the teachings of great religious leaders out into the streets and marketplaces and give them substance—our failure to comprehend the need for a living brotherhood—is pushing the peoples of the world, against their will, into a major conflict. We are stockpiling the materiel of war because we have not learned to recognize the material of peace. If we earnestly desire a peaceful world in which civilization can continue to grow, the American masses must hold firmly to the conviction that the practice of democracy in this country is our most powerful weapon against dictators and aggressors anywhere in the world. Only a practical and direct revelation of brotherhood can bring to us and bind to us the confidence and cooperative friendship of the peoples of Africa and the East.

In my judgment many of our strained international situations may be traced to our constant sidestepping of democratic practices in relationships with other races and peoples of less powerful countries. We have allowed our brotherhood to become obscured by offensive paternalism. As a nation and too often as individuals we have tended toward disdain in appraising the abilities of other nations. We have expended too much time and energy trying to fit the laws of God into our selfish desires, instead of leading people to accept and support the full implications of spiritual brotherhood.

As populations of the world grow in variety and number, do we hope to live—without reducing ourselves and other nations to the level of denizens of forests, ready to spring upon each other with regard only to might? It is better that we develop a common purpose with all nations and people. Within this are the blessings of a living brotherhood. Without it we shall reap the bitter fruits of brotherhood denied. I like to think that we in America have minds and hearts that are bigger than the formalities and hesitancies of protocol, and big enough to embrace as brothers the people and representatives of any friendly nation, whatever the population mixture.

The roots of brotherhood lie in the knowledge that unseen millions of our neighbors just beyond our shores have traveled with us the hard road to freedom. The open and sufficient warnings of jittery, distrustful nations, we brush off as *bluffs* because we cannot really conceive of any minor, undeveloped country standing up to us and intending to go through with it. We brush off the idea that people whom we deem culturally inferior might become scientifically superior. We attempt to work out reasons why countries with which we are in physical or ideological conflict should move in one direction instead of another. We then proceed to base our actions on our projected logic—forgetting that it is the product of our minds, not theirs. This comes from a fundamental failure to understand the concept of brotherhood. Failure to recognize the possibility that there are other ways of thinking which we must try to understand and deal with. Other abilities that we must learn to respect and deal with.

It is useless to expect Russians, Hindus, French, Italians, or Chinese to behave like Americans. And it is entirely possible that when we hold such expectations and insist upon conformity with our ways, we make people unhappy with us, resentful of us, and rebellious toward us. We seem to be having a difficult time with our statecraft or diplomacy. I wish that along with our departments of state and defense, we might have departments of human relations devoted to applying the doctrine of brotherhood, undiluted, to both domestic and international affairs.

Brotherhood is a word that strikes a responsive chord in our hearts. It is not merely a sentimental catchword; it is a reality which we can ignore only at great peril. The brotherhood of man is more than a slogan; it is the fiber from which democracy is woven. We Americans have accepted this brotherhood as one of our guiding principles. But democracy does not live by principles alone. It lives by practical application of principles in the lives of the people. Democracy is a way of life. It is a way of life that depends to a large extent on our acceptance of all people as *brothers* no matter who they are or what they are. We shall preserve and develop this democracy of ours only by living out the consequences of our belief in our brotherhood under God. We look forward to Democracy and Brotherhood.

# Reconcile

IN AMERICA WE HAVE NOT SUFFERED much. We have been free from the horrors of war waged on our own soil. We have not known the terror of shells falling on our cities, maiming men, women and children. We have not had to hide in the bowels of the earth, from the terror of death in the air. For this we are deeply thankful. But we may not always be so spared. The hour is here for Americans to look circumspectly, and band themselves together to help bring about reconciliation of the nations of the world.

Laborers, teachers, preachers, business people, college students— every American who can think at all—let us realize our responsibilities, assume them gladly, and share in maintaining a free world.

# Revive Humanism,
## Know and Respect All Nations

IT IS IMPORTANT FOR [AFRICAN AMERICAN] youth to become interested in the great struggles taking place in Asia and Africa. Our young people will live in a day in which colored peoples of the world will contribute the leadership which will bring these things to pass. Youth must know the peoples of the world. They must thoroughly understand that long periods of colonial rule, color prejudice, religious fanaticism and international inequality are responsible for the attitudes of the greater percentage of the world's population. They must know too that never again should a common bond of friendship among nations be based solely on the color of the skin. That the key to international relationships is personal relationships, based on mutual respect among nations.

There must be a revival and sustained evolution of humanism and humanitarianism, if countries are to mutually enjoy peace and prosperity. There must be a kind of spiritual grounding which nurtures friendship, understanding, and equality of approach. The day is past when pacts and treaties can be counted on to solve problems and resolve conflicts among nations. We live in times when tolerance and real understanding must take the place of pacts and treaties. As a race, we must unite our unique spiritual resources and put our spiritual strength to work with a new objective, with conscious purpose and a sense of historic perspective. Spiritual reawakening is the one thing that is most needed in the world today. Every element in our national life should be evaluated in terms of spiritual values. The modern world can have no place for anything that degrades the human spirit. At long last the human race has come to know that peace among nations can only result from righteous intent and intelligent action—but at the bottom of all intelligent action, there must be righteous intent.

# Know Right from Wrong

IN THE REALM OF HIGHER EDUCATION, we have finally discovered that a college or university is merely a place where young people are trained to achieve personal satisfaction and social usefulness. And we know that neither can be achieved without the capability of distinguishing among values: knowing that some things in life are better than other things; knowing that some things are wrong and lead to ultimate damage of the human spirit; knowing that some things are right and make life happier for all people. This may sound like a religious idea. And it is. We have learned that an educated person can have no social usefulness without some kind of religious sense.

It must be an intelligent religious sense. Not the kind of religious sense demonstrated by a city official not long ago who, when talking on *Americanism*, said: "We believe that the American way of life is white, protestant supremacy." The official proceeded with a vicious metaphor: "If you are born in an oven, you are not necessarily a biscuit." That kind of religious sense comes from a confused mind as well as a false sense of values.

In the field of education we have learned that educational practices now obtaining in the greater part of our country violate our democratic beliefs and threaten our democratic stability as a nation. We have learned that the waste in human resources created by segregation in education is the type of economic folly a democracy can ill afford.

We have learned that the practice of wrong does not bring peace. That people cannot long do wrong and feel right...until every phase of our society is set straight in the fulfillment of those divine potentialities which reside in every human being. A great moral renaissance is required—one that is spearheaded not just by educators but by the organized and effective power of the Church.

# Choose Knowledge over Ignorance

AS WE FACE OURSELVES AND OUR world, great and formidable barriers in several fields of action arise before us. Some are of greater significance than others. Some bind us physically, but these are not so forbidding as the barriers which inflict us with economic, social and spiritual bonds.

We face great barriers of prejudice, injustice and inequality—these intangibles which build imaginary walls among people, walls that cannot be easily moved or torn down. Doubt and distrust weld the walls, and fear so poisons the minds that people fail to venture with reason, fail to learn to probe their prejudices and do away with them. We face the barrier of ignorance where vision is darkened and lack of knowledge brings heavy shadows which obscure the light of truth. We need to discover a way to work that will unfold our vision and help us find the powers that come with ideas and facts and the relationships these develop.

Because of prejudice and a lack of sound education for our masses, we find ourselves face to face with the greatest barrier of all: the barrier of economic insecurity for the common man. In order to remove this barrier, we must have united efforts and consecrated leadership. We are called upon as never before to unite the energies, efforts and faiths of the human family so that a world community may emerge and a spirit of unity may encircle the entire earth.

Leaders around the globe are calling for a true translation of the ideal of democracy, because they realize that in a democracy there are vast spiritual resources which foster unity and the development of human potential. Are we sure that our democracy can be placed in the world framework and bring about peace to all who seek an answer to the social evils that surround them? We need most seriously to unite our strengths in order that the strong may definitely help to bear the infirmities of the weak. We need a united leadership whose combined vision will focus on the grassroots of societies' afflictions and bring courage and confidence. Eyes that are now dull and lifeless can be illumined when their hopes are rekindled; ears deafened by the blasting of bombs and painful cries can be opened to hear the inspiring messages from science as it renews health, from art and creative skill as it opens opportunity for self expression, from industry or invention as it shows how worthy is the dignity of man.

We cannot solve big problems with a few scattered individuals; we the people of all creeds, colors and classes must look forward to real unity in a united world family and extend through our combined influences the spirit of helpfulness to those who stand in need. We must live together, work together, and be willing to use the great measuring rod of justice and fellowship with people, for the sake of humanity everywhere. Let each one of us resolve to be a part of great social planning, so that our world may be freed from barriers of injustice, ignorance, economic and emotional insecurity.

127

## Choose Better over Worse

THERE ARE TIMES WHEN I AM amazed to hear many of our white citizens speak of America's problem of discrimination and segregation as something that has to be handled with *kid gloves*, with a sense of delicacy. Over and again, they say we *must not rush things*.

They speak as if time is something that itself works apart from the will and courage of the human spirit. I do not believe this. I believe that *time* is an area of eternity in which man has the will for better or for worse. If that exercise is in keeping with the highest ideals that man knows and to which he has given his collective allegiance, then man resolves his actions in keeping with Divine Will. And all his subsequent paths lead to peace and good will and understanding. On the other hand if that exercise runs counter to man's preachments, then resultant actions lead to physical and spiritual suffering. This seems self-evident to me. Centuries of history have proved it.

Today as a people we stand again in the same historic position of many great empires, cultures and civilizations of the past. The basic sources of trouble are the same. The same basic methods of force and overextended explanation are being tried as in times gone by. And many of the little yet great souls of the countless humble people throughout the world watch with fear of the outcome. They watch and yet they hold to the highest ideals that humanity has come to know.

I think of the great good that could be done in our own country if many of our leaders would approach segregation and discrimination with moral courage and a spirit of devotion to what they know is right and just. How my heart grieves for my country and my southland when I see the world looking at us in wonder as we debate the legal justice of segregation. How I pray that my country and my southland will see that peace is not won by the exercise of power nor by any exercise that runs counter to what we as a nation preach in the great halls of world assemblies.

## Rise Beyond Race

THERE NEVER WAS A TIME IN history when we felt more in need of courageous leaders for world peace: leaders whose philosophy is so simple, profound, and universal that all who read may learn and understand. Leaders who have risen beyond race, creed, class and color. Leaders who are committed to moral rearmament which makes our religious beliefs effective, broadens and unites us, and takes away the fear of war and destruction.

I am of a race that has suffered much from the perils of hate, injustice and slavery. And I have yearned for freedom from these things that separate and tear us down. Above all the peoples of the world who stand sadly in need of the ideology of Moral Rearmament, the peoples of darker races are most in need—for they have suffered so much. These are days when we are called upon to give all the encouragement and stimulation—that there will be no more war and hatred, but a great change of heart and action in all of us that will illumine the world.

## Hunger for Spiritual Growth

RELIGION IS ONE OF THE FIELDS of human experience. It is a phase of human conduct. A personal attitude toward the world in which one lives. Whatever a person's religious beliefs, they profoundly affect the life he lives. Religion constitutes one of the most vital elements in the secondary growth of humankind. Some people call this maturity the *growth of the soul*. Some refer to it as the *development of personality*. Others call it the *development of social responsibility* or the *development of social awareness*. It has been called by many names through the years. But in the early days of my life I came to know it as the simple fact of *becoming a Christian*.

As the years have gone on and I have watched thousands of young people grow up, I have seen that along with physical growth there invariably shows through each young man and woman a surging thirst after spiritual growth—that stops in the early years of their lives. When this happens the soul begins its slow but sure decadence. Many things are responsible for this. But in very few instances can the cause be dissociated from the adults who have the opportunity to affect the young life.

Many colleges have developed strong religious emphases and have realized an institutional product that stands up throughout all the demands and vicissitudes of modern life. But getting a vital religious life into the collegiate community is something more than *rules and regulations*. Young people cannot be coerced into *religion*. No person, young or old, can be made to believe that a person's attitudes toward his fellow man or his conduct in association with the ends he seeks in life are the very heart and core of human happiness. This idea has to be made alive. And on the collegiate scene the idea has to be surrounded by teachers and administrators whose lives show forth a dedicated standard by which young people may see the truth and become caught up in its powerful appeal. Such an ideal campus would not be a dull, uninteresting or unhappy community. It would be an exceedingly alive and happy college. It would be a campus of Christians. And real Christians do not carry their religion. Their religion carries them.

It is not a weight but a buoyant power. It lifts them, it sees them over hard places, it makes the universe seem friendly, life purposeful, hope real, and sacrifice worthwhile. It sets them free from fear, futility, discouragement, and all the great enslavers of the soul. People are happy as they become inwardly free—as they grow in the spirit.

## Be Morally Mature, Don't Hate

THE MOST PRESSING, MOST VITAL COLLECTIVE moral problem of our national life is segregation, discrimination, and organized hatred. The ramifications of the problem reach far beyond national boundaries. Racism is at the core of every international problem today. Although it has economic and political overtones, the problem itself is essentially and primarily one of moral maturity. Many church people recognize this and are conscious of the Christian's responsibility in the matter. But current efforts lack cohesion and organization. The forces of evil unite, while the forces of righteousness preoccupy themselves with individual interests and petty differences. Isolated skirmishes with evil cannot effectively combat an organized army of evil.

There are new movements emerging which have all the earmarks of other national movements which were organized for and thrived on race hatred and persecution. The new movements use the same appeals as the older but well-known *hate campaigns*.

Why is it not possible for the church to organize the forces of righteousness? Why is it not possible for the church to organize a national association for the advancement of Christian living? What a wonderful thing it would be to see the good people of the country working together in a common bond of love and fellowship—working together to establish the Kingdom of God on this earth. I already envisage what kind of organization it would be. It would emphasize the *spirit* of religion, rather than a form of worship. It would emphasize the necessity for the inner person to grow in righteousness, so that the outer person might express and live that righteousness. It would cut across lines of denomination, and biblical interpretation, and theology. It would concern itself only with the goal of denominations. It would be made up of all people who abhor the evil of hate, all people who earnestly desire to establish the rule of love.

I am greatly saddened by the picture I see of those who defend the existence of segregation and discrimination. These defenders are described as people of importance: some of them as specialists in constitutional law, one of them a former candidate for the high office of president of the United States. They are described as speaking before the Supreme Court in voices "choked with emotion." They are quoted as predicting suggestive consequences to the [African Americans] if the Supreme Court decides "against" segregation in the public schools. Their arguments are amazing, for one sees the nature of their emotion. It is the tremendous undercurrent of hate-tinged feeling.

All of this is very disturbing because it shows warped attitudes. A state of spiritual illness. It confirms one of the major criticisms leveled by our enemies against our "Christian civilization": namely, the terrible hypocrisy of the Christian religion as it is practiced in so many communities of our country. It foreshadows the decay in national morality, a decay which can become malignant if the better thinking,

134

better "Christianized" people of our country do not face up to the great shame of our century.

The failure of the church to meet its responsibility in the matter of racial discrimination and segregation is the great shame of our century. This problem being tried before a high tribunal on a legal basis—has waited for many, many years for a decision before the high tribunal of humanity's religious convictions. The question reflects legal aspects, but the problem itself is incontrovertibly a moral problem. The time has come for the spirit of humanity to become free. Segregation holds captive those who defend it. It beclouds their thinking. The choked emotion of their voices is but the cry of their immortal souls straining for freedom from the debasing effects of racial bigotry.

These people are dangerous. Their attempts to deny complete freedom to all people by circumventing constitutional guarantees is a serious matter in a country like the United States. Their preachments veer too near the attitudes which were prevalent in Nazi Germany prior to World War II. The world harvested the whirlwind of devastation which followed in the wake of Nazi racism. What started as carefully perverted logic ended in the slaughter of millions of people and a condition of worldwide unrest, suspicion, and subtle hatreds which live even to the present day. It is disturbing, therefore, to know that we still have people in our country who are the proponents of the very ideas which have in one decade cost the world more blood and tears than history has ever recorded. These people who defend segregation in "voices choked with emotion" are not only dangerous, they need help. They have done and thought *wrong* to be *right*. They need Divine help.

This is why the church must feel responsible for racial bigotry. When the consciences of so-called *responsible* citizens become deadened, when their lives make a mockery of fundamental religious precepts, then the church can no longer feel comfort in silence. Such silence leads to spiritual death.

# Defeat Force Without Force

THE REAL PATRIOTS OF AMERICA WILL always be alert to threats against [the human] *spirit*, whether those threats come from within or without.

[But] our country today is exposed to a dual threat. Our so-called *cold war* has two fronts. And the fight is made much more difficult because of evil men who threaten from within. A part of the cold war is the fight against people who seek to perpetuate the evils of racial discrimination and segregation within the boundaries of our own country. These people are enemies of the United States. Unwitting enemies, but enemies nonetheless.

Those among us who seek to preserve the spirit of our land and make of it a real and living code of conduct reflecting itself throughout the world must face up to this internal disaffection. It is an unpleasant task because it is always disturbing and saddening to be compelled to chastise or criticize our brother. But when his preachments and actions would destroy our home, continually humiliate and debase our citizens and thereby hold our country up to world ridicule—then our brother must be criticized and chastised. This does not mean that our country has to be split again in a spirit of vilification or persecution. Name calling and unjust punishment have no part in the moral code of patriots.

In our struggle we must use every instrument of morality and law to persuade our unfortunate brethren that America has come of age in world affairs. To do this we must continue to maintain a sense of understanding and perspective. But we must grow in moral courage. America has become physically great because of her ability to envisage *bigness* and perfect long range planning. Our country can become spiritually great by means of the same vision. We must see the bigness of our job in combating spiritual *littleness* at home. Our social institutions should play an especially important role in this planning, for one of the main difficulties involved in the complete national maturity of our country lies in the discrepancies between ideas and the collisions between beliefs. They have to be mediated and reconciled. This will of course result in an enlargement of our personal horizons and a new view of ourselves in a world of diversified cultures and critical appraisals.

We cannot solve the problem by meeting emergency situations. We cannot solve the problem by creating apologetic Sundays. The time has come when some responsible institution like the whole church, not a mere division or creed, must unite with every other social, economic, and political agency in the land—not for the purpose of nationalizing religion, but for the purpose of implementing those teachings which are the foundation of our political and religious structures.

The time has come when America must mobilize her spiritual resources. We must do this if the "American Way of Life" is to take on any real meaning to foreign ears—not to mention the millions of second class citizens at home. If and when the church takes up the fight to free the American scene from the suicidal afflictions of racial segregation and discrimination, the American people will find themselves engaged in one of the most significant social enterprises in the history of the human race. This enterprise will be significant because, although it will defeat the dangerous philosophy of force, it will involve none of the elements of force. It will be significant because it will come to grips with the basic problem around which all current political ideologies revolve. It will be significant because it will remove the onus of national hypocrisy with which our country has been plagued ever since our spokesmen for social justice have attempted to speak in world assemblies. It will be significant because the church will have placed itself on the side of the *doers* of good, not merely the moral proponents of social justice.

I believe that the major responsibility for such a task lies at the door of the church.*** I believe this because the issue of segregation and discrimination (by virtue of the color of skin and a former cast condition of legalized slavery), is basically a moral issue. Segregation and discrimination in practice may resolve themselves into political or even legal questions. But in essence they involve the moral sense of our country. And moral problems of this kind the church has too long evaded and outrageously sanctioned by its silence and evasion. The religious life of our country must in itself be a healthy life before we can expect morality to pervade all avenues of life which have to do with humanity's complete spiritual and physical well-being.

# Don't Just "Stand For," Do

THE PEOPLE I FEAR MOST ARE not the communists, left-wingers, or crackpots. I fear the good people who believe the right things, belong to the right things, but who never do anything about it. They just stand for the right things; they never move in and help push these things along.

This statement sums up just about all that can be said about America's great moral problem of segregation and discrimination. Almost without exception, every responsible writer, speaker, and leader in public life agrees that our country faces a choice between *practicing what we preach* or having all our efforts in world affairs come to naught. The time has come when America must do more than *stand* for the right. America must do something about what is right. In the long run it does no good to fight wrong unless the one who attacks wrong also lives right. This is our vulnerable spot in our dealings with the communists. This is the moral cancer that we must cut out of our

139

national life. It is costing too much in lives and money. It costs money to practice a national sin.

It is appalling to realize the millions of dollars that have been wasted in this country in an effort to maintain the illusion of the inequality of races. It is even more appalling to realize that this money has been spent by communities that *stand* for democracy and Christianity. The part of our country that has spent more millions than any other section of the country in order to maintain segregation is that part of the country where the loudest protestations of Christianity are heard. The whole story of segregation and discrimination is a recitation of inconsistency and compromise of conscience. Today that compromise is a tool in the hands of our enemies. We have molded a weapon more powerful than any bomb the genius of man may devise. We have placed that weapon in the hands of the enemy. And it is costing us billions of dollars. It costs money to tolerate a national sin.

What is the remedy? We already know the remedy. We have known it for centuries. As a matter of fact we *stand* for the remedy. It is now time for all the good people who stand for right to begin doing something about the practice of right.

Women's groups have taken a stand on segregation for a number of years. But we have reached the stage in our moral growth that we must do more than take stands. We must do more than pass resolutions. We must do more than condemn. We must do more than say a thing is wrong. We must take positive and affirmative action for the right. We must practice what we say is right. This is not a job for organizations alone. It is an individual job for every man, woman and child in every part of our country.

I believe the Christian church should be the leading light in this movement to free America from the shackles of shame. It should occupy most of the time and attention of the church. It is a moral problem. Just as it is true that a country cannot live half slave, half free

—no country or part of a country can practice racial persecution and, at the same time, practice Christianity. The two are opposites. They are inconsistent. One makes the other wrong. They cannot be separated in the living process.

If Christianity is right, then racial discrimination and segregation are wrong. If Christianity is right, then racial humiliation and persecution are wrong. If Christianity is right, we cannot go on making a mockery of [it] by the way in which we practice [its] teachings.

Let us *stand* for the right, but let us also be up and about God's business on this earth. Let us live the life of Christ.

---

Chapter 6 NOTES:

*In his January 6, 1941, State of the Union message to the Congress, President Franklin D. Roosevelt said: "In the future days, which we seek to make secure, we look forward to a world founded upon four essential freedoms. The first is freedom of speech and expression—everywhere in the world. The second is freedom of every person to worship God in his own way—everywhere in the world. The third is freedom from want—which, translated into world terms, means economic understandings which will secure to every nation a healthy peacetime life for its inhabitants—everywhere in the world. The fourth is freedom from fear—which, translated into world terms, means a world-wide reduction of armaments to such a point and in such a thorough fashion that no nation will be in a position to commit an act of physical aggression against any neighbor in the world." Ref: *Respectfully Quoted*, The Library of Congress.

**The year before Mary McLeod Bethune died, she was an invited guest at the World Assembly for Moral Re-Armament in Caux, Switzerland. Ref: Thomas and Smith.

***Bethune explained further her use of the term church. She said she used the term in a universal sense. "I include three major religious convictions of our country: Catholicism, Judaism, Protestantism. I do not condone, criticize or attempt to explain any of the aspects of creed or theology. I point out one thing and that is that these three faiths all believe in the dignity of the human individual, the possible divinity of the human spirit, and the common relation of all men under one expression of Divinity. This in itself is enough to bring these three together in a timely, definite effort to firmly establish the dignity of the individual in the practical avenues of everyday living."

# Power Faith with Activism, Hope

*THE COMMENTARIES IN THIS BOOK ARE informed by Mary McLeod Bethune's American experience reaching back as far as Reconstruction and as close as World War II, the Korean and cultural conflicts, the Red Scare, and the early years of the Cold War. Bethune's commentaries, of which her* Chicago Defender *columns were the most prolifically recorded, are her firsthand account of struggle and challenge, responding to events of her day. These writings are imbued with strains of hope and humanity woven through hundreds of speeches, sermons, discussions, and writings for America. Never before have her verbatim thoughts been compiled and offered to a general adult audience.*

*In her eighty years, Mary McLeod Bethune sustained all the hurt, humiliations and indignities of anyone born [African American] and female in America. Her response to hurt, humiliation and indignity was action, advocacy, activism, creation.*

*She embodied a faith and love and hope that transcended meanness, hate, ignorance, fear and adversity. She knew the America that revealed itself in the actions, reactions and prejudices of Americans in general and [African Americans] and women in particular—she knew them well. But she believed firmly in America's founding principles, in the spirit of America's people, in the divine inevitability of the rule of righteousness.*

*On this foundation she lived and hoped and gave of herself in love and service to humanity. Hers is a portrait of hope, a counsel to hope in these troubled times when terrorists scares and hunters have replaced Red scares and Red Hunters.*

*"There should be no misgivings or lack of hope," Mary McLeod Bethune said. We need not doubt the intrinsic nobility of the human spirit or God's ultimate salvation of the spirit.*

*"There is no reason to let up, no excuse for becoming complacent, no room for despair. The forces of freedom are rising. Truth will not down. It will free itself, however great the pressure against it."*

## Meet Challenges

ONE OF THE MOST CONTROVERSIAL PROBLEMS of our times was underscored one day when a bomb was dropped on a voting place to frighten [African Americans] away from the polls. Our schools were just beginning to turn out more eager youth, ready to enter into full citizenship. The bomb did not slow up the voting. Young and old turned out that day in larger numbers than ever before. They knew that their right to vote had been challenged, and the challenge had to be met. The strong roots of progress and brotherhood had reached far down into the soil of our democracy—too far to be killed by smears or bombings. I am given new zeal, new courage and greater faith as I watch once more a great expression of Americans marching forward together.

# Fight Americans' Injustice
## with America's Justice

THIS IS A LAND WHERE A man is judged not by his name, not by his ancestry, not by his creed, but by his ability to produce and his eagerness to get along with his fellow men.*

This is a marvelous statement. And although there are many closed doors in industries, housing outrages, violence, police brutality—we know such actions are not *in the American tradition*. We know they contradict American concepts of freedom and democracy and the rights we would free and protect from the last, tenacious grip of feudalistic thought and inroads of totalitarianism.

We know that in these United States we can fight injustice together as the crew of the Flying Enterprise fought the sea together. Despite bombings and brutal slayings "by law," despite flaming crosses, lost jobs and all other manner of intimidation—which I have witnessed in my day, we can move ahead through the orderly procedure of the courts and through the power of growing friendship and understanding and devotion to the American tradition.

# Stop War

IN ALL MY YEARS AND WITH all the tragic drama of war I have seen pass across the great screen of history, I have yet to find any sign that the human race has finally come to believe that war is a pestilence among nations; and persecution of one's neighbor is also war, though on a different scale. That until we learn how to treat individuals we will never dispel the notion that war among nations is necessary. There is no sign of moral growth toward the spiritual resurrection portrayed by Thomas.** Yet there are some things which may be called *signs*.

I would like to believe that the United Nations is a sign that man is learning the ways of peace. I would like very much to believe this. Yet I know there is much that makes the great work of the United Nations ineffectual. Perhaps we are in a period of growth and these great expectations will come to pass in after years. I hope so.

I would like to believe that the great wave of conscience that is sweeping the world is a sign. People everywhere are becoming articulate about the great wrongs of racial and economic exploitation, segregation and discrimination. I would like to believe that even this constitutes a sign that we have done enough wrong to believe we should start doing right.

# Take Advice of Good Ancestors

IN THESE DAYS WE ARE REQUIRED to find a sense of balance for the many shocks that come to us perforce. We are required to have a sense of inward poise, enabling us to cope with any news story, however devastating. We are challenged to meet the difficult and trying experiences of the day, whether they are on a purely personal level or whether received as a conscious citizen of the world. We are challenged to meet these experiences with faith and fortitude and with a transcendent outlook which makes possible a smile in response to a frown, love where hate is expected, forward movement when backward movement seems inevitable, faith in the realization of one great world when enemies all around demand our surrender. For every weight placed upon us, there is a balance. It makes no difference what happens that is wrong, unjust, or unfair—sufficient minds will be opened, throughout the United States and the world, to think and do something tangible about it. There may be martyrdom in order to unfold some

149

blatant injustice, shocking enough to arouse the conscience of those who sleep. Dramatic incidents awaken drowsy, indifferent minds and inspire to even greater courage those who have fought long and hard and fearlessly.

Young citizens in the making, be not discouraged by what may appear to be overwhelming disasters of the present day; try to catch a gleam of the fortitude and determination of those who have given you a demonstration of courageous living—those who have been building the bridge with only you in mind, the bridge upon which you now stand. Regard yourselves with spiritual and moral vigor and join in the fight down to the last ditch for that democracy and peace and justice which belongs to you and to all humanity.

## Call on Divine Help

YOU WHO DWELL UPON THE FERTILE plains of life and others who eke out a bare existence upon the rugged slopes of the mountains —today we are facing tremendous world problems. The atmosphere in which we live is a charged one. Confusion, stress and tension are humanity's most common companions. And the plaintive pleas of millions are heard as they totter upon the precipice, hoping they will not fall into the abyss of destruction. What steps should be taken to achieve peace, safety, and security? Our failure to answer this question adequately could well mean the prelude to a symphony of annihilation.

It seems strange that the human race has moved from one level of existence to the plane which we now call civilization, yet is unwilling or unable to make the right step when the next step could bring total destruction.

The lessons from the pages of history and the combined wisdom of contemporary leaders are not in themselves adequate to meet the situation which confronts us. Neither will the resolute spirit of the masses be able to sustain us. Hence we must summon a force greater than humankind in this dark hour of world strife and conflict. The time has come to attempt to reach beyond our previous reachings and to implore help from the Divine Spirit who never fails. Our wisdom is too fragile, our decisions too indefinite. We cannot meet the situation alone. We must now if ever call upon and rely upon our different forms of petition and worship to the God who can give life and sustain us forever.

# Break the Chains

NOT ONLY HAS THE [AFRICAN AMERICAN] been in chains of servitude, America herself has been in chains. But both the [African American] and America are beginning to break the most powerful shackles that have ever bound humanity. America wants to be free to join both black and white keys in great Amens, that will swell from the organs of human understanding. This can happen if men and women will look upon the world with vision and imagination and faith. I ask women to use their minds, their faiths, their strengths toward perfecting a great unity, getting placement on national and international frontiers, and leading the land we love to its rightful place of spiritual leadership in a world that is seeking peace.

Unity is the answer to our needs and hopes. And it seems certain we must pay a price in one way or another. Naturally there will be struggle and sacrifice. There will be disappointments and troubles. There will be valleys and seeming darkness before the noblest ideals can be attained. But following the *troubles I see*, there is *Glory Hallelujah*.

I thank God for America, a land in which change and progress can be implemented for the sake of ideals we cherish. I thank God I am a champion of future successes because of what I have seen. I know one day other leaders will look out upon a world where human beings of all kinds will have justice and good will and peace. To that end I challenge you to unite, to work, and to serve your day.\*\*\*\*

# Give No Quarter

Living dedicated lives: Brooking difficulties, discouragements and prejudices. Forging ahead with the gifts given by God. Having faith in the impossibilities of the times, faith in the ultimate goodness of humanity, and faith in yourselves. Knowing the tasks, trials, temptations and tempestuous transitions of eventual history and remaining captain of your soul—without asking or giving quarter, and vanquishing the foe of an earlier time and changing the countenance of America. Seeing new horizons and leading the hopeless and defeated to that light—these are the keys to progressive change, and to ever-evolving tomorrows. There should be no misgivings or lack of hope.

# Take Stock, Keep the Faith

IT IS FITTING AND PROPER THAT we take stock now and then—of the progress we are making, of the changes in attitude, of new champions entering the field of battle on the side of right and justice. Such inventory strengthens us for the struggle yet before us. It heartens those who may begin to think we are fighting hopelessly. It is no sign of weakness to acknowledge progress. It is strategic. It is smart.

First-class citizenship is still not within our grasp. But while we have not yet grasped the victory banner, we can see it now on the hilltop. We have all the more reason to climb over the rocks, ford the streams, hack through the jungles and keep moving forward. The road back is no longer any tougher than the road ahead. We must keep moving forward to a brighter tomorrow. Indomitable courage, undoubted sincerity, unfailing faith—of these three qualities—the greatest is FAITH.

I know from my own life of more than seventy years of sacrifice and toil that he who has an abiding faith has more than riches, more than worldly power, more than an army at his back. In all the years of my struggle—matching wits with adversity, prejudices, discriminations, unequal opportunities both as a woman and as a Negro—I have never wavered in my faith. When I started my school, now Bethune-Cookman College in Daytona Beach, Florida, materially I had only $1.50, the use of a lean-to on a dump heap and a few wooden boxes. But I had an unlimited supply of faith. When I began dedicating my life to the improvement of our American way of life by urging and insisting upon extension of its full benefits to all Americans regardless of race or religion, I walked into many doors that were solidly bolted and walls that seemed unscalable. I was often told there wasn't a chance of success; that I was wasting my time. I was sometimes urged to devote my energies to less hopeless tasks. At times, the darkness was so impenetrable I was tempted to turn back onto paths whose turns and hazards were familiar to me. But I held on to my faith. I kept pressing forward.

Today more and more of those doors are being unbolted and thrown open; those walls are crumbling section by section. While it is true that the problem of civil rights, particularly as it affects [African Americans] in America, is far from solved, it is encouraging to note the increased interest and determination on the parts of many groups to do something about it. Based upon the tenets of Christianity, the Church should be in the forefront of such interest and determination. Much yet remains for the Church to do.

Principles of brotherhood, neighborly love and justice verbally taught—have been no match for patterns of discrimination legally entrenched. But the doors will open and the walls will crumble—and they will do so because of our faith.

Yes, I appreciate the tremendous power of faith. There is no stronger force in the world today than Faith. But in my abiding faith—I have never been one to sit back and wait for manna to drop from heaven.

In her Last Will and Testament, Mary McLeod Bethune said this:

"…Yesterday, our ancestors endured the degradation of slavery, yet they retained their dignity. Today, we direct our economic and political strength toward winning a more abundant and secure life. Tomorrow, a new [African American], unhindered by race taboos and shackles, will benefit from more than 330 years of ceaseless striving and struggle. Theirs will be a better world. This I believe with all my heart."*****

---

Chapter 7 NOTES:

*English poet Samuel Taylor Coleridge, 1772-1834.
**From Biblical Scripture Thomas, an apostle of Jesus. Ref. John 20:24-29.
***From Biblical Scripture: "Then he answered and spoke unto me, saying, This *is* the word of the Lord unto Zerubbabel, saying, Not by might, nor by power, but by my Spirit, saith the Lord of hosts." Zechariah 4:6. New Scofield.
****Bethune again echoes Coleridge's poetry: "Work without hope draws nectar in a sieve, and hope without an object cannot live," 1826.
*****Reproduced in Audrey Thomas McCluskey and Elaine M. Smith, eds., *Mary McLeod Bethune Building a Better* World, Indiana University Press, 1999.

# Selected Chronology

Mary McLeod Bethune 1875-1955

*Outstanding leader of black women from the 1920s through the 1940s.*

1875:         Birth: Mayesville, South Carolina.

1895:         Teacher.

1898:         Marries and continues as teacher.

1899:         Becomes mother and continues as teacher.

1904:         Founds Daytona Educational and Industrial Training School for Girls in Daytona Beach, Florida [concentrates on educating girls, later black women]. Opens mission schools for railroad workers' children in eastern Florida.

1907:         Faith Hall built at Daytona Educational and Industrial Training School for Girls [Later Bethune-Cookman College].

1909:         Supports NAACP. President National Association of Colored Women's Clubs.

1911:         Opens the McLeod Hospital with two beds. WW I Helps raise funds for American Red Cross.

1920:         Leads vote campaign despite Ku Klux Klan opposition.

1923:         Raises curriculum from elementary to college at Daytona Educational and Industrial Training School for Girls [later Bethune Cookman College]. Student population 600 students; more than 30 teachers.

| 1923: | MMB becomes a founding director of Central Life Insurance Company of Tampa, Florida. |
| 1924: | Travels to Europe. |
| 1929: | Bethune-Cookman becomes co-ed college, emerges from girls' school. |
| 1930: | Serves on President Herbert Hoover's Child Welfare Commission and Conference on Home Building and Home Ownership. |
| | Other local Daytona community institutions built: hospital for blacks refused service, mission schools for loggers' children denied schooling. |
| 1933: | Heads Minority Affairs Division of National Youth Administration under President Franklin Roosevelt. |
| 1935-1949: | Founds and leads National Council of Negro Women to address needs of colored women and girls. President of National Association of Colored Women and National Association of Teachers in Colored Schools. |
| 1936: | Heads Association for the Study of Negro Life and History & Carter G. Woodson's Publishing House. |
| 1935: | Receives Spingarn Award given by NAACP for highest achievement. |
| 1936: | Directs Division of Minority Affairs, National Youth Administration under President Franklin Roosevelt. |
| 1936: | Only woman in a group of FDR advisors called the Federal Council on Negro Affairs, or Black Cabinet (McCluskey and Smith, 1999).        Receives Frances A. Drexel Award for distinguished service to her race. |
| 1940: | Made history forcing Johns Hopkins Hospital (Baltimore, Maryland) to allow black doctors to observe her sinus operation. Writes newspaper and magazine columns primarily for the Black Press. |
| 1940: | Vice President of NAACP. |

1941:      Loaned by NYA to be special assistant to Secretary of War to aid in selection of Negro women officer candidates for Women's Army Corps.

1942:      Resigns presidency of Bethune-Cookman College.
Receives the Thomas Jefferson Medal from the Southern Conference for Human Welfare.
Anti-discrimination protests: speaks at Madison Square Garden.

1943:      Bethune Cookman grants first college degrees (MMB is 68 years old).

1943:      Women's Army Corps advisory committee service continues.

1944:      Tours European installations, argues for racial integration in Women's Army Corps.

1945:      President Harry Truman appoints MMB to founding conference of United Nations (observer at initial conference in San Francisco). Advises President Truman.

1946:      Resumes presidency of Bethune-Cookman (1 year).

1949:      Rollins College (Winter Park, Florida) grants honorary Doctor of Humanities Degree to MMB, first awarded to an African American by a Southern White college (McCluskey and Smith).

1952:      Emissary to West African country of Liberia.

1952:      Only woman president of an insurance company in America (Central Life Insurance Company of Tampa).
Writes for black publications: *Chicago Defender*, *Pittsburgh Courier*, et al. throughout her life.

1954:      U.S. Supreme Court rules in Brown v. Board of Education of Topeka.

1955:      On board of Planned Parenthood & other national organizations.
Life ends May 18, 1955.